EYES V

HELP!

with

Control Freak
Co-Parents

Debra A. Wingfield, Ed.D.

ISBN-13: 978-1495479908
ISBN-10: 1495479900

Cover design and book graphics by Jeff Leader

Cover art by Debra Wingfield

Photos by Diane Hammerland

Debra can speak to your group or organization through the magic of technology. Call 1-719-647-0652 or email info@houseofpeacepubs.com

Disclaimer:

I am not an attorney. This book is based on my research, training, reading extensively the literature about the Family Court and Custody Disputes, Child Custody literature, and Empowerment Advocacy work with Protective Parents and their children. Since the majority of Protective Parents are mothers, the book is written based on this gender language. If you are a Protective Father, simply change the gender language as you read the book.

Seventy per cent of Protective Parents lose parenting time with their children when the abusive parent demands primary parenting time or sole parenting time through Family Court litigation.

This book is not designed to meet the therapeutic needs of the reader. However, this may be a useful book for you to use in therapy with your psychotherapist.

This book can help attorneys, mediators, judges, and mental health professionals understand the non-physical dynamics of domestic violence identified as Coercive Control.

A portion of the sales of this book will go to CourageousKids.net

What others are saying

Know His Tricks and Be Strong
By Dr. Erica Goodstone

This is an amazing and much needed book that is a first step toward making huge change in the way we view relationships. Many of us have a starry-eyed perspective, believing that "he" (and sometimes "she") can't really be that bad. Even the abused partner, the victim, who may have been subjected to abuse for a long time, even that person may secretly believe that it can't be that bad, that something must be wrong with "me."

This book provides intricate details of the words and tricks and manipulative actions that determined abusers often use to get what they want and how they sometimes manage to fool their friends and even the court system. Women need to read this book to help themselves remain strong and to possibly assist a friend or relative who has become an abused victim. Men need to read this book in order to realize that their power-over gig is ending and that it is time for them to seek help or to reign in their male friends and relatives who are abusive perpetrators.

Very Helpful and Informative --- easy to read and understand
By Michelle Mueller Carter

I found this book Extremely helpful and informative. It is very easy to read and understand, and it kept my attention. I definitely can relate to it. I highly recommend this book to everyone. if it does not fit you and your life chances are there is someone you know who could benefit from this book. Please let others know about EYES WIDE OPEN: Help! with Control Freak CO-parents ..... especially Judges, Lawyers, and Law Makers

An Important Book Teaching Tricks of Manipulation
By Ronda Del Boccio, The Story Lady

Chances are that everybody knows or has known someone who is in an abusive relationship. The abusers use so many sneaky, subtle tricks to manipulate their spouse. This book by Dr. Debra Wingfield reveals the various tactics and tools of coercion that are being used against them.

This book is important because the health and safety of children and abused spouses is at stake every day. Please gift this book to anyone who is struggling to get free of an abusive relationship.

Ronda Del Boccio
bestselling author, mentor and speaker

A call of action - please pick up an extra copy of this book and give it to a family court judge in your jurisdiction!
By A. Sokolova, J.D., MBA

Dr. Debra has created an enormously important tool that can potentially save thousands of lives from very preventable forms of abuse. As society we have been ignorant to what has been happening in the family court system and how it affects our most vulnerable people - children.

This book is a life offering born out of complete dedication to the subject and unconditional love to every child and every parent who dared to stand up and speak up. It helps those parents better understand the reality they find themselves in, and navigate through it to a safer harbor with the least damage.

Educate yourself and pass the knowledge on !

Other books by Debra Wingfield, Ed.D.

From Darkness to Light: Your Inner Journey

Through a Child's Voice: Transformational Journaling

Available through
HouseOfPeacePubs.com
Products link

This book is dedicated to all protective mothers and fathers who want to keep the Family Court out of their relationships with their children.

ACKNOWLEDGMENTS

Thanks to Dr. Suzanne Larsh for help with review of the assessments. Thanks to Cyndia Pace, M.A. for her helpful editing. Thanks to all the mothers and fathers who permitted me to share their stories. Thanks to all my friends and colleagues who provided support and feedback throughout this project. A special thanks to my husband, Charles, who patiently listened to all my rants about what is happening to children removed from the safety of their protective mothers and fathers.

The Story Behind the Story

Dr. Debra Wingfield has worked for more than 40 years counseling and training in the Interpersonal Violence field. Her work includes providing counseling with all age groups who have experienced domestic or interpersonal violence and abuse. Her professional training courses cover abuse across the lifespan.

Beginning in the early 1990s, Dr. Wingfield started working with victims of domestic violence in her private counseling practice. The domestic violence field was still very young and there was limited research or discussion about how to help domestic violence victims. She used her experience in working with abused children to help her identify what was most helpful to these women (primarily) and sometimes men. At that time, she noticed that domestic violence was just a part of the continuation of abuse across the lifespan.

After completing her doctorate, Dr. Wingfield started working with domestic violence offenders as well. She learned what brought them to this level of offending and wanted to stop the abuse cycle by intervening with offenders. By gaining a broad picture of what makes offenders behave abusively in their relationships, she was better able to help their victims make decisions for safety for themselves and their children. All this work was primarily connected to the criminal justice side of domestic violence.

In 2010, Dr. Wingfield came face-to-face with how domestic violence abusers were using the civil justice system, through the family courts, to gain custody of their children. This experience prompted her to do an in-depth study of this part of the Interpersonal Violence field.

In her advocacy work with protective parents (primarily mothers), Dr. Wingfield endeavors to empower protective parents to continue to protect the well-being of their children. She provides emotional support and referrals to resources. She provides feedback on how protective parents present themselves to the court and court-appointed professionals. Dr. Wingfield recommends helpful tools that support survivors to become thrivers.

If you would like Dr. Wingfield to review your case, contact her through **questions@houseofpeacepubs.com**.

Debra A. Wingfield, Ed.D.

CONTENTS

Section I
Co-Parent with a Control Freak

Reality Checks

Section II
Control Freak Tactics
Know your Voice

Reality Checks

Section III
Control Freak Tactics in Family Court
Stop your voice from being Silenced... Again

Reality Checks

Section IV
Control Freak Tactics with Physical and Sexual Violence

Reality Checks

Section I
Co-Parent with a Control Freak

Protective mothers who leave abusive relationships may think they are leaving the abuse behind. They are unprepared for the abuse to continue especially if there are children from the relationship. Courts want children to have relationships with both parents as much as possible. Only through providing judges with behaviorally specific descriptions of abuse during an intimate relationship can we start to protect children after their parents are no longer a couple. With the present court system asking parents to co-parent after separation and divorce, the protective parents (primarily mothers) need tools to help them continue their parental relationship with someone they may consider a "control freak".

Debra A. Wingfield, Ed.D.

Reality Check #1 **Find Your Voice**

This guide helps protective mothers keep the Family Court out of their relationships with their children. In 2010, I focused my work in domestic violence toward empowering protective parents (primarily mothers) to maintain relationships with their children and work toward their well-being.

Some of the cases noted in this book come out of that work. None of the cases uses any identifying information to protect the children and their parents. Several themes continue to be present in the cases and in other situations where I read about protective mothers battling courageously for the sake of their children. After hearing many stories of protective parenting from my clients, these are the repeated issues that I know protective mothers encounter:

> **Losing parenting time with your children**
> Being cut entirely from the lives of your children
> **Being sent to jail for attempting to protect your children**
> Being sent to therapy for "alienating your children from the abusive parent" when the abusive parent is actually alienating the children through his own actions.
> **Being sent to "reintegration therapy" after children were removed from being parented by their protective parent.**

Other examples of coercive control covered in this book, where protective mothers are seeking other options outside the oversight of the courts

What is Coercive Control?

Coercive control tactics are patterns of behavior designed to maintain power and control over a partner or children in a relationship. A co-parent who used coercive control tactics during your relationship is likely to use those same controlling behavior patterns with you after you separate or divorce. There may be small differences in how coercive controllers use coercive control tactics after you are no longer living together. However, they do not change their behavior just because you leave.

The domestic violence field is shifting from the terminology "power and control" to "coercive control tactics". The purpose here is to move away from the mistaken notion that domestic violence is only seen as physical abuse. By using the term "coercive control" or "coercion and controlling behaviors or tactics", we are able to expand the dialogue and describe in behaviorally specific terms the nature of the abuse. When coercive and controlling behaviors are assessed using a frequency measure, we are able to document repeated patterns that the abused partner experiences.

This is important because there are two viewpoints in the literature. One is that men and women are equally abusive with their partners. The other is that men are the primary abusers. The literature that supports men and women being equally abusive toward each other is based on survey responses that focus on situational violence.

The literature from assessments of victims seeking safe shelter from their abusive partner shows these are primarily male abusers and females who are abused. The means to assess the second group use tools that ask about frequency and severity of abuse and violence. This literature goes beyond physical violence to look at coercive control in the relationship. Thus, showing on-going patterns of specific behaviors that have some level of predictability for being repeated.

Family Court Philosophy

Since the family court philosophy is for the child to maintain a relationship with both parents, in *Eyes Wide Open: Help! with Control Freak Co-Parents*, you are provided with the knowledge to identify the Coercive Control Tactics that are repeated patterns your ex-partner used during your relationship and may continue to use since your separation/divorce.

You are provided tools you can use to effectively protect yourself and your children in order to keep your situation from being labeled "high conflict" by the courts. By using these tools, you may be able to reduce the risk of a multitude of professionals involved in your family's lives, making recommendations about parenting and determining when, where, and how you will co-parent.

The book is divided into four parts. The first part is a general discussion of the problems and issues Protective Parents find as they move through the separation and divorce process in Family Court. The second part covers the various Coercive Control Tactic Patterns used within relationships and after the relationship ends. The third part of the book covers the Coercive Control Tactic Patterns occurring in Family Court. The final section discusses physical types of abuse that include sexual coercion and physical violence.

Feel free to skip to the sections that can be of most help to you immediately, then take some time to go back and read the whole book. The time put into completing the assessments and doing the Transformational Journaling™ Focus Points™ can be immensely helpful for you as you continue to come across the coercive control tactics while you move forward on your life journey.

If at any time you need help to understand a specific coercive control tactic or pattern, feel free to contact me at **questions@houseofpeacepubs.com**.

My goal is to help you set healthy boundaries with your co-parent in order for you to live a life filled with joy, happiness, and peace.

Dr. Debra

Reality Check #2 **Games Control Freaks Play**

There are four motivations and 12 coercive control patterns plus 3 patterns specific to family court we will review together. In addition, you have an opportunity to go through a series of checklists to help you identify the coercive control tactics that were used by the abuser in your relationship. You can determine how those coercive control tactics are now being used to maintain control of you after you left your relationship.

After you identify which tactics currently are being used, you can use the Transformational Journaling™ tools described in the next chapter to release the emotional charge tied to the coercive control tactics used. Then, you will be able to respond instead of react to your coercive controller co-parent. This process is what I use when I consult with protective mothers to help them maintain safe boundaries for themselves and their children.

Before we get into setting safe boundaries, let us review the four motivations that coercive controllers use to pull you into relationships with them. They use these same motivations with their attorneys, any court-appointed professionals assigned to your case, and with judges. This is what makes it so difficult for these professionals to understand what you are attempting to tell them when they have not seen the coercive controller shift from the sweet, nice, personable man you first met to the abusive man who came out after you were taken hostage. He does not show this side of himself to professionals in legal proceedings. The four motivations coercive controllers use to manipulate and control other people are:

Cunning
Conning
Convincing
Charming

Four C's of Coercive Control Tactics

Through my work with protective mothers and working with abusive men in batterer intervention/treatment programs, I identified four motivations abusers use to maintain coercive control in their relationships. These four motivations are often the red flags that women miss when they are drawn to an abusive male. Why?

Because abusers know they must keep their abusive behaviors hidden in order to lure a woman into a relationship (take them hostage). Therefore, the mask the abuser uses is very thin, and he can only maintain these four motivations that underlie coercive control for a short time.

This is why women have whirlwind romances where they end up moving in with the abuser or marrying him very quickly. Otherwise, the relationship falls apart and he must go out and hunt down another woman (hostage). Let us look at the four C's:

> **Cunning** abusers lull you into a sense of security and safety. They do this by letting you know they will protect you and make sure you are safe from any outside harm. What they do not tell you is that *they* will be the source of harm to you in the future. They are just waiting for you to tell them how much

you love them and only want to be with them for the rest of your life.

Conning abusers show you how wonderful they are and that you are now forever in debt to them for rescuing you from your previous "awful" situation. Abusers con you into believing that they really love you and that you are the only one for them.

Convincing abusers reinforce what they have conned you into believing about them. They will lie and exaggerate to "make you feel" that you "want to take care of them" because they have been hurt or abused themselves. They appeal to the "rescuer" in you and say they understand what you have experienced in prior abusive relationships or with your parents because the same thing happened to them.

Charming abusers know how to say and do "all the right things" to feed into your fantasies of being cared for, loved, and, nurtured. He buys just the right presents, brings flowers at just the right time, and woos you until you convince yourself he will always treat you as special. He counts on you falling under the spell of romance as described in all the books, songs, and movies that end with the couple "living happily ever after."

Do these motivations make sense to you? If so, you may find yourself laughing or smiling right now as you realize this is what happened to you. You may also feel sad or embarrassed that you bought the package the abuser was selling. Remember, you are not alone. Abusers are very well-trained by society and family to engage in these motivations to "win you over." The real key is to make sure this never happens to you again.

Debra A. Wingfield, Ed.D.

Reality Check #3 **Your Roadmap to Healing**

How to protect yourself

Now, let us begin your journey to heal from being in a coercive controlling relationship. You are given empowerment tools with Transformational Journaling™ exercises to help you heal and keep yourself from being drawn into the web woven by the abuser in the future. In fact, you will more likely find that you start spotting abusers before they even get near you and find yourself running as fast as you can the other way to avoid them.

By now, you are probably asking yourself, what is Transformational Journaling™? This is a journaling process I developed when I was recovering from abusive relationships. It is designed to help you identify what is happening with the abuser and how to keep yourself emotionally and physically safe from him. The tools you will adopt to take responsibility for yourself and to keep your children safe are provided so that you can continue to use these tools for the rest of your life.

Transformational Journaling™

This is an excerpt from the book *From Darkness to Light: Your Inner Journey*, the first book I wrote about Transformational Journaling™. It is available on the

HouseOfPeacePubs.com/products.htm website. In my experience, the best way to achieve maximum results is through written journaling. There are many ways to journal, including using the journaling *Focus Points*^{TM} throughout this book. If you prefer to use your computer to write your journal, I suggest you put it in a password-protected file. You can keyboard or use a voice recognition program to write your journal on your computer. Various voice recognition programs are available.

Another alternative is to speak into a recording device. The disadvantage to this method is you miss seeing what you have put down. You are less likely to go back and listen in the future. By having written words, you have an opportunity to go back, read, and identify patterns in your thoughts and feelings. You can learn from these patterns and make conscious choices for change.

Some people get stuck on writing because of concerns about spelling, punctuation, and grammar. Set aside your concerns because this journal is for you. If you choose to share it, you will probably do so verbally. In my journal entries, you will notice incorrect grammar and punctuation.

Another set of questions I am asked when I recommend journaling are related to how often to journal, when to journal, and how much do I journal? My response is to find a quiet place and time of day when you are least likely to be uninterrupted. Set aside 10 to 15 minutes daily as you learn these techniques. You may choose to journal for a longer time period. However, establishing a set time and location is the process for building your journaling muscle. Reflect on your day and find what works best for you.

When I first started journaling, I found the first 10 to 15 minutes before bedtime worked best for me. This is my relaxing and unwinding time to read before going to sleep. Adding journaling for the first 10 minutes gives me time to reflect on my day. Find what works best for you and establish a daily journaling pattern. So, relax, enjoy the journey, and let your words flow.

Throughout this book, you will find ***Focus Points^TM*** (in *italics*) to give you a taste of journaling. My suggestion is you buy a special notebook or bound journal for your Transformational Journaling^TM. Remember, healing is a journey. Take time to nurture yourself as you move through the process. You did not get to this point overnight. You will need whatever time it takes to recover from the abuse and coercive control you have experienced.

Debra A. Wingfield, Ed.D.

Reality Check #4 **Grow Protective Children**

Empowerment Tools to Help Your Children

You recognize how precious your children are and the nurturing, caring, and love they need to grow and develop into strong, self-responsible adults. You know a tree needs water, food, and nurturing to grow and remain healthy for many years. As a parent, you focus on providing for and nurturing your children from the time they are a growing embryo throughout their childhood and even through their adult years.

Part of your role as a protective parent is to make sure your children are not subjected to trauma and stress that is outside the normal range of human experience. You do this by watching them closely when they are young to make sure they are safe. You teach them how to keep themselves safe as they venture alone into the world. You guide them to make responsible choices for themselves as they grow into adulthood. Your goals are to guide, nurture, and help your children develop into contributing members of society. You want to help them create healthy families and feel good about the lives they lead.

You never expect them to be put in harm's way physically, emotionally, sexually, or through neglect. When traumatic events do occur in their lives, you want to be there to comfort and nurture them through it. This teaches your children that even if something hurts or disturbs them, they will be cared for and nurtured.

Types of Stressors

As a mother, you have an instinctual drive to keep your children safe. Now, research tells us why—because stress from traumatic experiences increases risk of early onset (mid-forties to mid-fifties) for mental and physical health problems. This extensive research on the impact of stress in the lives of human beings shows three major types of stress.

These types of stress are managed in different ways that are explained below. The management of stress allows children to continue positive growth and development when parents are there to help them. If parents are unavailable to help their child manage the stressors they encounter in their lives, the impacts can have lifelong adverse consequences.

The three types of stress human beings experience are: 1) positive stress, 2) tolerable stress, and 3) toxic stress.

Positive stress is something we all want to have all the time. This type of stress represents the positive feelings we experience as we go through the many situations presented to us on a daily basis. For example, walking outside to just stand in the sun and enjoy feeling the warmth on our bodies creates a positive feeling inside us. When children receive hugs, praise, and nurturing from their parents, this is positive stress. This is a positive stressor because the body experiences a reaction to this behavior. The reaction of the body may be a slightly elevated heartbeat and changes in hormonal levels.

You may be asking yourself why I included hormonal levels. In addition to the sex-based hormones, the body produces other hormones that have various functions to keep us alive. The hormone connected to stress called cortisol is secreted from the adrenal glands. It controls: 1) proper glucose (sugar) metabolism, 2) regulation of blood pressure, 3) the rate that insulin is released for blood sugar maintenance, 4) controls immune system functions, and 5) the body response to inflammation. All that is a big mouthful to say our bodies depend on cortisol to keep us in balance.

The second type of stress is tolerable stress. Again, this type of stress is something we experience throughout our lives. Tolerable stress is our response to an adverse experience that is mildly to strongly threatening to our well-being. For children, this may be a visit to the doctor's office where they are placed on an exam table, undressed, and examined by a stranger. The child (infant) does not understand what is going on; however, mother is there to soothe the child and tell the child who this stranger is and what the doctor is doing.

Another example of tolerable stress is when a child falls down and may have a skinned knee that starts to bleed. The child runs to mother for comfort and have the knee bandaged. The tears from the immediate experience of the pain are dried up, and the child feels soothed and nurtured. The stress reaction is reduced and the child runs off to play again.

The third type of stress is toxic stress. The child experiences this type of stress when an adverse experience occurs and no adult is there to provide comfort and nurturing. The child is left to *self-soothe.* The length of time this takes puts added pressure on the adrenal glands to continue working longer and harder.

When a child experiences continual adverse toxic stress situations, these experiences drain the body from the ability to produce sufficient cortisol to keep the body in balance. Research shows these types of continued adverse toxic stress events result in the early onset of physical and psychological chronic health issues.

Some of these are depression, heart disease, and addiction to drugs and alcohol.

Factors related to toxic stress include: all forms of child abuse and neglect, witnessing mother being treated violently, having a parent out of the home due to incarceration or institutionalization, and having a parent who abuses drugs or alcohol. The more factors that occur in a child's life, the more likely they are to have early onset chronic illnesses.

What happens to our bodies when we are continually put under toxic stress? The body uses up all the stress defense mechanisms, which causes the body to age more quickly. This means we start developing chronic diseases at an earlier age than anticipated by the medical community. These chronic diseases include heart disease, cancer, diabetes, obesity, etc.

The body experiences a lowered resistance to fight disease, and the effects are seen when physicians start seeing patients with chronic diseases at younger ages, as early as mid-40's to mid-50's. This is hard to believe when people are staying healthier longer and living longer. However, this may not apply to adults who had adverse childhood experiences that were significantly traumatic and are carried in their bodies.

A person who has experienced toxic stress in childhood is likely to have trauma-related physical and emotional issues. How does this happen? First, an abusive parent who is supposed to nurture and protect the child betrays the child's trust. Then, the betrayal feelings stay in the body long after the trauma is over and continues to be felt at the physical level.

The good news is there are many ways that promote healing the physical and emotional wounds of adverse childhood experiences. If you want to know what options are available for your particular situation, please contact me at questions@houseofpeacepubs.com.

Here is what you can do as a protective parent. Help your child build resiliency skills and take advantage of their strengths. This accomplishes some of the healing. We will talk about these in more depth later in the book.

Children's Developmental Stages and Toxic Stress

Different types of stressors have a direct influence on children's developmental stages. Children experience different developmental stages physically, emotionally, socially, educationally, morally, and spiritually. A child's parents, teachers, and other adults in their lives nurture and guide each type of development. We have markers of the different types of development.

Annual visits to the pediatrician or family doctor help the parent monitor the physical development of their children. Height, weight, and overall body functioning are the focus of these visits. Additionally, the doctor checks on the social, emotional, and, educational development of the child by asking the parent how the child is doing in school, whether the child is developing friendships, and how the child gets along within the family and the community.

Parents are more directly involved in the spiritual and moral development of their children. Parents transmit their values, behaviors, and actions around the child. Parents may choose to involve their children in religious education and attendance at a church, synagogue, temple, or mosque, or spiritual organization. These groups support the parents' choice of moral and spiritual values to pass onto their children.

How does toxic stress impact development?

Children exposed to toxic stress often show stunted development emotionally and morally in adolescence and adulthood. Often, this is seen when young adults are put in situations where they are expected to use good emotional judgment and they make poor decisions due to lack of emotional maturity. These decisions often are coupled with poor moral choices as well.

In their relationships, young adults who were exposed to toxic stress may feel like they are playing catch-up with the maturity levels of their peers. They may be more super-responsible or more irresponsible than their friends and co-workers. Super-responsibility may be a cover-up for their low self-esteem while irresponsibility may be acting out their low self-esteem issues.

Mental health therapy can help a person recover from the effects of toxic stress and catch up with their peers developmentally. In therapy, repairing the impacts of toxic stress takes approximately one month for every year since the toxic stress occurred to the current age of the adult child. For example, a child who began experiencing sexual abuse at age 9 and comes to therapy at age 32 carries the effects of toxic stress for 23 years. Therapists guesstimate that it will take almost two years of therapy to repair the damage of the emotional, social, and moral effects of toxic stress experienced in childhood. These adults may never feel like they catch up with their peers.

From the standpoint of physical impacts, the ACE (Adverse Childhood Experiences) Study showed the long-term physical effects of adverse childhood experiences. These experiences create toxic stressors in childhood that begin to manifest in the mid-40's to mid-50's age-range with the early onset of chronic illnesses. Thus, it is very important to prevent children from exposure to toxic stress whenever possible.

Why is it important to understand the impacts of toxic stress when co-parenting with an abusive ex? Because you are in a position to provide this information to your attorney and the court-related professionals in your case, and you can ask your attorney to bring in expert witnesses to detail the damage your children experience with toxic stress. Ultimately, this may have an impact on how Family Courts address the Best Interests of the Child standard in the lives of your children.

To learn more about your children's developmental processes to help them reach their maximum potential, go to the "Child Development" web page of the Centers for Disease Control and Prevention (see resources in Appendix B or HouseOfPeacePubs.com/resources.htm. Make sure that what you read is based on scientific research. Look for the author's qualifications and the peer-reviewed research they used to develop their information.

Standards to Live By

What are standards to live by? These are the basic rules you establish about what is acceptable and what is intolerable in your life. You might think of this as the line you will not cross. How much room do you allow your children for exploration and discovery of their world? Of course, this is definitely a developmental process based on children's ages.

Young children are watched more closely than older children. For example, young children haven't learned to watch out for cars, to see if it is safe to go into the street to recover a ball that went outside the yard. Older children know that cars can be dangerous and they must look before walking into the street to get a ball back.

What are the standards you set for yourself and your children to live by? How do you define those standards? In what areas of your life have you established standards? What is important to you? What are the limits you set for yourself and your children? What is acceptable behavior? What is intolerable behavior?

These are all questions to ask yourself and write about in your journal. When you know the answers to these questions, then you are free to apply them to your life and your children's lives. This establishes the standards you live by.

Beliefs to Follow

There are many types of belief systems tied to the eight areas of life I recommend you examine in your Transformational Journal™. There are beliefs about who you are as a person and the characteristics you want people to see in you. These characteristics have to do with your identity, your attitudes, and your behaviors that are stable over time.

The beliefs you have about what is good to have in a relationship partner, in relationships with friends, and relationships with family are all part of the attitudes you express through your actions toward people you are familiar with as well as strangers. You may have learned idealized beliefs from movies, songs, and books that are not based in the reality of your daily life. These beliefs often change over time as we grow personally and have a multitude of life experiences.

While writing this, I noticed an article in "Dear Abby" by a woman who was waiting for "Prince Charming." This particular fairy tale belief often runs smack into reality when women realize "Prince Charming" is just that—a fairy tale character. In my journal, I wrote many pages on how I would become my own "Prince Charming." As I listed the characteristics I put on this character, I realized I was very capable of providing for myself all that I thought "Prince Charming" would bring into my life. This allowed me to give up this dream and live my life on my terms.

Relationships are very complicated. When our internal compass is off track, it is very easy to be pulled into a relationship that does not reflect our beliefs. If our beliefs about relationships were distorted while we were growing up, we may have a history of picking partners who are not healthy for us. We may need some time to correct our distorted thinking before we get into future relationships. For all relationships, we may need time to fix our "picker."

Your picker is what draws you to certain people and sends you running as fast as you can away from others. Your picker is like an antenna that brings in information about another person and tells you, "This person looks interesting and I would like to know them better." Or, your picker may send up "red flags" that say this person is someone to stay away from. If your picker is broken, it is worth the time it takes to fix it. Then, you have a chance to pick someone who is actually there for you in a relationship rather than there for themselves.

Part of fixing your picker is starting out slowly with meeting people and making friends. You can do this in safe places, such as support groups. Here you can meet other people who are re-evaluating their lives and want to experiment with new skills. They may be working on how to make friends, how to have effective conversations, or just how to be themselves.

Since you are not making a lifetime commitment, you have a chance to talk freely with confidentiality being agreed to within the group. In other words, no one talks about what is said in the group outside the group. No one talks with one group member about another group member. Your group goal is to use this place as a safe haven to try out new ideas, new behaviors, and express your values without judgment. There is no reason to stay connected with any group member when the group disbands.

This type of support group can be found in various locations. Sometimes counseling centers offer these types of groups, churches often provide support groups, and self-help organizations offer these groups. Today, you can find these types of groups online on social media sites, or in online forums, and blogs. Be careful about who has access to information in online groups so your ex does not have access to your posts. These can be used against you in court.

Values to Teach

Values and standards often overlap. Values are what our children learn from watching what we do and how we treat other people. Values include showing respect to adults and children. Some common values are being honest, being loyal, being kind, being respectful, taking responsibility for one's actions, getting a good education, being courteous and polite with others.

Character Counts is a program used in schools to help children gain positive values for life. It focuses on six pillars for strong value systems in children:

Trustworthiness

Respect

Responsibility

Fairness

Caring

Citizenship

These values are foundational and are just part of the values we want our children to adopt. Beyond these values are a long list of other values children learn while they are growing up. In the eight areas discussed in this book, your Transformational Journaling™ will focus on those values.

Why teach values? To help children grow up to lead productive and satisfying lives. When you are clear about your values (which may or may not reflect those of your parents'), you will teach those values directly and indirectly to your children. You will teach them directly by explaining your values to your children. You will teach values indirectly by your actions and behaviors observed by your children.

Here are the areas recommended for you to consider when reviewing your standards, values, and beliefs:

> **Character values, standards, and beliefs**
> Relationship values, standards, and beliefs
> **Family values, standards, and beliefs**
> Recreation and Social values, standards, and beliefs
> **Spiritual values, standards, and beliefs**
> Educational values, standards, and beliefs
> **Career values, standards, and beliefs**
> Financial values, standards, and beliefs

You will receive some Focus Points™ to help you clearly identify your standards, values, and beliefs at the end of this chapter.

Help Your Child Develop Resilience Skills

What is resilience? Why it is important to child development? Resilience is the ability to bounce back from adversity and keep moving forward in life. When a child falls down while learning to walk, we comfort the child and encourage him or her to get up and try again. This adult response helps the child build resilience to keep working toward his or her goal of walking easily on his or her own. Your role as a parent is to encourage your child, which builds resiliency.

25

The child is learning even from this early age the benefits of making more than one attempt to achieve an accomplishment. When they are knocked down by life circumstances, they get up and go for their goal again and again. One of your goals may have been to have a successful relationship and/or marriage. When you were knocked down, you stuck in there and tried to make it work. Even though you were fighting a losing battle with a coercive controller, you still tried to make it work. That is a resiliency skill you have.

Another area that helps us understand and provide healthy development for our children are the Developmental Assets. These assets are identified in a study done at Search Institute in Minnesota. Researchers identified 40 assets that helped children face adversity and still become healthy, productive members of society. The more assets a child has, the more they are able to handle adversity and have positive life experiences.

The increased assets actually prevented children from getting involved with alcohol and drugs, teen pregnancy, and violence. The more assets a child has, the less likely they are to engage in these risky behaviors. The Search Institute found that parents and other important adults in children's lives can help children develop these assets.

Developmental Assets Support and Build Strengths

Here is a brief overview of the 40 Developmental Assets. Eight categories divide the Development Assets. **The four external asset categories are:**

Support
Empowerment
Boundaries and expectations
Constructive use of time

The four internal asset categories are:
  Commitment to learning
  Positive values
  Social competencies
  Positive identity

When parents intentionally build these assets in their children, they are creating resilience skills and building strengths that help their children thrive throughout their lives.

You can learn more about the 40 Developmental Assets by going to the Search Institute's website. The link is in appendix B or on the HouseOfPeacePubs.com website in the Resources link.

 Right now, I want to focus on how you intentionally build Developmental Assets in your children. Some asset building is done directly by talking with your children. You encourage your children to experience various situations, or teach them what is important to you and help them learn your values, standards, and beliefs.

For example, if you want to teach your child the difference between telling the truth and lying, you might create a game with them where you say something outlandish that they know is untrue. Then you ask, was I telling the truth or lying? Children age seven and above are able to tell the difference between the truth and a lie. Be prepared for your child to test you with the same game just to see how it works. This makes it fun for them because they get excited to see if they can stump you. Remember, always be truthful with your children to help them understand this value.

Asset development occurs indirectly when children see what you do and hear what you say. That is why it is so important to remember that telling a child "do as I say, not as I do" is a very unhealthy message.

For example, if you want your child to avoid using tobacco products, illegal drugs, and alcohol, then you must talk to them about your beliefs in this area. Also, you must live your beliefs. Having a parent-child chat while you are smoking and drinking a beer clearly gives your child the wrong message. Now, I am not saying you should avoid smoking or drinking alcoholic beverages. You must know that the message you give should match your behavior in the situation.

Children will challenge your use of tobacco products and use of alcohol. You need to be prepared to educate them about different choices for adults and children. Also, children are likely to follow the behavior of their parents, so it is important to decide what you want them to learn from you.

This is true of relationship behaviors as well. We know from research that children who grow up witnessing domestic violence and coercive control are more likely to have relationships where those issues are problems. Some studies found boys are more likely to repeat their father's behaviors and girls are more likely to repeat their mother's behaviors. Your choice to leave an abusive situation is also a lesson you teach your children.

You can empower your children further by teaching them what is wrong with abuse and coercive control. You can also teach them healthy ways to be in a relationship. One book that focuses on these issues is *From Darkness to Light: Your Inner Journey* (http://houseofpeacepubs.com/products.htm) by yours truly.

Reality Check #5 **Control Freak Communications**

Communication Tools for a Protective Parent to Use with a Coercive Controller Co-Parent

From my work with coercive controllers and domestic violence offenders, I learned how to communicate with them to avoid their manipulative communication. We will go into the specifics of what to do and what to avoid. First, it is important for you to understand their motives behind their communications.

Coercive controllers have three goals behind their communication and their behaviors.

> **First,** they want to shut you up.
> **Second,** they want to stop you from doing what you want to do and force you to do what they want you to do.
> **Third,** they want to retaliate against you for something you have done to them or they think you have done to them.

Every time you respond to a coercive controller's messages the way he expects, he believes he has won. In truth, the coercive controller has lost because what could have been a good relationship is being ruined by his desire to have power and control over you. You are actually reacting with the goal of defending and preserving yourself, rather than responding. Your reaction creates the ammunition to escalate the situation to the next level until the coercive controller gets what he wants.

It is now time for you to learn to respond from a place of safety and confidence. This takes a little time to learn, so if it backfires the first few times you do this, keep working with the tools I give you. You will get the hang of it. If you feel stuck, just e-mail me your communications at **questions@houseofpeacepubs.com** and I will help you rephrase them.

Here are some basic rules to keep in mind when communicating with a coercive controller.

Rule #1: Stick to the facts, and only the facts.

Rule #2: Only discuss the issue at hand, never any other issues between the two of you.

Rule #3: Keep your emotions out of your communications.

Rule #4: To avoid having your buttons pushed, stick to the facts and stay away from the triggers the coercive controller knows from his past study of you that makes you the caring, empathic, person you are.

Rule #5: Talk with a safe, knowledgeable person (such as a therapist) about coercive control and domestic violence to express your emotional reactions about your ex and to get clear what is safe for you to communicate.

As you work through this book, I will explain Transformational Journaling™ processes for you to use to prepare your responses. Then, I will give you specific Focus Points™ to use to work through the five rules.

First a few words about communication and personality. Communication is a lot more than just talking or sending e-mail messages or text messages. It is all about the hidden messages behind the communications. When you are communicating with a coercive controller, they bury the hidden messages in their communications. That is part of their personality of looking good to the outside world. They want to hide who they really are until they are behind closed doors.

The theory of personality development that I like to use to explain this is Transactional Analysis. This was a theory developed in the 1960s by Eric Berne. Berne broke the personality down into three basic parts, the Parent, the Adult, and the Child.

A diagram that shows this is below:

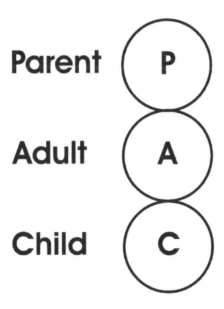

Parent (**P**)

Adult (**A**)

Child (**C**)

These three parts are in everyone's personality. They make up the whole of who you are. These three parts are also present in your partner or ex-partner. When you communicate with each other, you send your message to your partner from one part of your personality to one part of your partner's personality. This is called a Transaction.

In a fully functioning person, these three parts of your personality are closely balanced as in the diagram above. However, in my experience, I find many coercive controllers' personality parts are out-of-balance. They tend to have a very large Child part of their personality, a small Adult part of their personality, and a big part of the controlling Parent part of their personality.

It looks something like this:

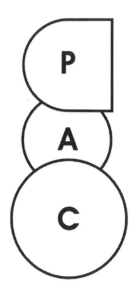

What does this mean about their personality? Generally, the coercive controller tends to have more of an attitude that everything should be about him. He wants all the attention, care taking, and nurturing. This can lead him to become jealous when you give attention to yourself, your children, your career, or your friends or other family. A coercive controller's focus is on meeting his own needs and wants.

How does this affect his communication style? He is usually communicating to you from his needy, wanting Child part of his personality. He wants you to be there only for him. The easiest way for him to accomplish this is to take you hostage and control you. If you fail to respond to his needy, wanting attitudes and behaviors, he just increases his coercive control tactic patterns until you give in and comply with his demands.

By now, you are probably wondering why he would even consider having children with you. Children represent his virility and manhood. In essence, he is saying to the world he is grown up and knows how to "act like it." The key piece here is he tends to act like a grown-up in public or among other family members, but act like a needy child behind closed doors.

When you leave a coercive controlling partner and take your children with you, you have taken away his image he is portraying to the outside world. Many coercive controllers only want custody of the children because it continues to perpetuate the image he is portraying. It has nothing to do with his desire to be a good, caring, nurturing parent. Just as you fight to protect your children, he is fighting to protect an image made of smoke and mirrors.

What makes communicating with a coercive controller so difficult? Since he is motivated to maintain his image, he communicates in ways to continue to keep that image. Your communication is based on protecting your children from harm. Since you are communicating from different goals, you are constantly crossing your transactions and he is working at cross-purposes with you.

How do you resolve these communication differences?

You need to remain in the Adult part of your personality when communicating. Stay away from the Child or Parent part of your personality. At the same time, you are attempting to shift the coercive controller communications from his overly needy, wanting Child to stay in his Adult part of his personality. That means you stick just to the facts, and keep all emotion out of your communication.

When he realizes you will only communicate around facts that relate to your children and that no matter how many manipulations he tries to pull, you remain focused on the facts, he will gradually stop baiting you. Be aware that he may seem to comply as a way to pull you back into his game, and then throw in a button-pusher or trigger of yours. By being aware of this, you will be ready when this happens and simply ignore anything that he communicates that is not about the facts of your co-parenting.

Here is an example of what this type of communication looks like when mother is attempting to find an agreeable parenting plan with father and protect her infant son at the same time. Communications occurred by text, e-mail, and with phone calls between mother and myself. Father diverted the focus of the conversation several times to keep mother intimidated just to give into him. I am just providing a sample of what occurred around negotiating parenting time for Thanksgiving.

Father sent the same e-mail several times while ignoring mother's responses because they were not to his liking.

In this example, all father's e-mails are copied to his attorney and the GAL. This is designed to make mother look like she is uncooperative. Father initiates the communication. Noted in "quotes" are the types of coercive control tactics the father uses.

Many protective mothers ask for help when they are attempting to respond to abusive e-mails and texts. This shows the decoding process. Mother's responses are in *italics*. **Readers if you want**

help to decode communications, please contact me at questions@houseofpeacepubs.com.

An example of how to decode control freak communications

Father approaches mother via e-mail about Thanksgiving break parenting time. There are two separate issues because one of the children is a one-year-old infant. The two older children have been on a 5-2-2-5 schedule that has not allowed mother one full weekend with the children since the first court hearing in February. Mother's attorney (her third) since the case began suggested a 2-2-3 (Monday-Tuesday, Wednesday-Thursday, Friday-Saturday-Sunday) schedule several months prior to Thanksgiving so that mother and father would have every other weekend.

[This schedule is on a two-week alternating basis. Parent 1 has the children Monday and Tuesday, and Friday, Saturday, and Sunday in week 1. Parent 2 has the children Wednesday and Thursday in week 1. For week 2, parent 2 has the children Monday and Tuesday, and Friday, Saturday, and Sunday. Parent 1 has the children Wednesday and Thursday. This is considered a 50/50 parenting time schedule.]

Mother, through her attorney, and through the court-ordered co-parent communication educator, has attempted to get the 2-2-3 schedule in place. Whenever it comes up, father throws in all types of conditions that prevent an agreement from occurring to keep mother from having all three children together. This is consistent with his behavior in the marriage. Father would not allow mother to have all three children with her at one time. This was part of his "isolation tactics" to keep her from visiting her family and friends.

In the first e-mail, father reminds mother that the judge said she wanted holidays shared 50/50. Mother asked me if I remembered the judges' statement.

Advocate by phone to mother: I checked my notes and the judge did order 50/50 for holidays. She did not clarify what she meant by this order.

Mother's first response to father (Advocate helped mother word her responses based on mother's decisions):

> *"I will agree to starting the 2-2-3 schedule for [older children] beginning November 18.*
> *Exchanges when school is held would be at [their school] at 3:30 when school ends.*
> *Exchanges during school breaks would be at the public Library at 3:30 on weekdays.*
> *All Friday exchanges would be at noon at the library.*

Father's second e-mail where he numbers each point.

Father agrees to 2-2-3 schedule, and then in later e-mails he fails to acknowledge his agreement. Instead, he accuses mother of not agreeing to the schedule. (This is gas-lighting behavior, a form of "emotional abuse".)

Father states the dates he will have the children and the dates mother will have the children. Father is treating mother as if she is not able to figure this out without him spelling this out. This demeaning behavior is "emotionally abusive".

Mother already agreed to the change in the parenting time schedule. She just spelled out the exchange times and locations in her first response.

Mother sent me a proposed calendar for November using parenting time software from an online website. The calendar clearly shows the 2-2-3 schedule with school day exchange times at 3:30 when school lets out.

Based on phone conversations with mother, this was her proposal for the infant.

Mother's second response:

> *Infant overnights: 2 nights each week on the 2-2-3 schedule not including Thanksgiving holiday.*
> *When you have [older children] for the weekend, you would have [infant] Friday and Saturday night.*
> *[Infant] would be returned at the library on Sunday at noon.*
> *When I have the children for the weekend, you would have [infant] overnight for Wednesday and Thursday the following week.*
> *This would be the schedule for this week and next week. You would have [infant] Nov. 19 and 20 overnight with a return time of 10:00 am on 21st. Nov 29 and 30 for 2 consecutive overnights.*

Father did not agree to the additional overnight during this week, therefore, he returned infant based on the previous schedule. Thus, he missed an offer by mother to have two consecutive overnights with the infant during this week.

Mother responds:

> *[Infant] would be with you Nov 29 from 3:30 when you pick up [older children] with 2 overnights returned on Dec 1 at noon.*
> *During the break, [infant] would be with you from 3:30 when you pick up [older children] for one additional overnight Nov 25 to 7:30 p.m. on Nov 26.*
> *[Older children] would be exchanged at 3:30 on Nov. 27.*
> *[Infant] would be with you from 4:30 to 7:30 on Monday and Tuesdays when you have [older children].*
> *On the regular 2-2-3 schedule [infant] would be with you for 48 hours on your weekends from Friday at noon until Sunday at noon.*

> *[Infant] would be with me all 3 days for my weekend.*
> *This schedule would continue after the break until final*
> *orders.*
> *All exchanges would be at public Library.*

Father already agreed earlier to exchanges at the public library when the court-ordered exchange center is closed. Since mother did not agree with father about changes to the infant's schedule, father demands that infant stay on the same schedule currently in place. This would keep infant separated from siblings during mother's parenting time. ("Isolation" of the children from the mother and from each other.)

Father agreed to pick up older children on his parenting time at the school. This would reduce some of the face-to-face exchanges. However, the infant would still need to be exchanged face-to-face or at the visitation/exchange center.

Father, also, agreed to the Friday exchange time mother suggested. However, he wants mother to pick up the children from his home when he has the children. This is a safety issue since father threatened to kill mother on more than one occasion. Father is dictating a change ("threats and coercion") in having exchanges at a safe location that has been occurring at either the library or the local exchange center as ordered by the judge. "Intimidation" and "threats" for mother's personal safety are the issues here.

Next e-mail from Father where Father is using black and white thinking to "intimidate" mother into doing what he wants. The advocate advised mother in a phone conversation not to give into his bullying behavior.

Father replies in his next e-mail:

> He states mother's proposal is not 50/50 and "threatens" her that he will just go through the lawyers.

Before mother can reply, father now starts making "threats" related to another topic.

Father ignores mother's earlier agreement to the schedule for the older children and attacks her for not agreeing.

Father "blames" mother for not doing what he wants without regard for her wishes.

Mother simply added exchange times and locations to clarify the agreement.

Father accuses her of making things too complex.

The advocate advised mother to insert her responses into father's email and return them to him. She put her responses in a different color to be clear that she was responding to father. Mother discussed her responses with the advocate before she put them in her return e-mail.

These are mother's responses:

I agree with 2-2-3 for [older children] and all exchanges at the main library. This is the third time mother responded with her agreement. Father's refusal to acknowledge mother's agreement is "gaslighting". Father is trying to make it sound like he is willing to negotiate when he is demanding ("verbal and emotional abuse") answers.

Mother's answer:

No. Advocate suggested. *This is my proposal which I sent to you earlier this week.* Note that Mother is learning to repeat exactly what she said previously until father understands that she will not give into his demands. This is an assertive communication technique.

I will only exchange children at the library, as it is a neutral public location.

Father continues to push his case that mother pick up the children from him at his home.

Then, father moves to negotiating parenting time with the infant above and beyond the holiday time. He wants two overnights a week and to maintain his current level of parenting time.

Mother has repeatedly said research studies do not support the infant having overnights. The custody evaluator also said no overnights for the infant until he is age five. However, the evaluator backed down on this at an earlier court hearing because overnights were already started.

Father does not acknowledge that mother has already addressed the issues of the infant's overnights in her first response ("Threats").

Father has not responded to any proposals mother has made. Father uses Co-parent Communication Educator as further "intimidation tactics" to force ("coercion") mother to agree with him. However, mother informed me that father rarely speaks up in these sessions, ordered by the court without regard to mother's safety. Mother has testified in court that she left after calling law enforcement because father threatened to kill her. It was not the first time.

Mother used advocate's suggestion:

I have provided several offers that you have declined. When my attorney returns to his office, I will review my current offer with him. Then, I will get back to you about [infant's] schedule.

Father continues to badger mother about the infant parenting time completely ignoring her initial response. ("Threats, coercion, intimidation").

Advocate suggested mother refer father to previous response on the next issue.

Father used another issue to "intimidate" mother to do as he wants. He continues his accusations that mother is keeping children home from school when they are with her.
Mother:

> *[Older son] was running a fever on Tuesday night through the morning. [Daughter] had diarrhea on Tuesday and Wednesday.*
> *Wednesday morning she also was running a fever. I put her on the BRAT diet during these two days.*

Father's final point refers to the custody evaluator's recommendations.

This is what mother wanted to respond.

> *If we are following Dr. [custody evaluator's] recommendations we do not pick and choose, if we do the most important is that there shall be no overnights until [infant] is 5. Holidays are laid out specifically.*

Advocate suggested: Your response could escalate this conflict. Change this to show what court has ordered regarding infant overnights. Also, you may refer to your earlier proposal for this holiday.

As mother's silent partner in helping her to communicate with her abuser, I was able to support her through these very abusive communications. At one point, mother wanted to give up. I encouraged her to stay strong.

As it turned out, father refused to bring the children to the library on Friday at noon. It took mother going to her attorney's office and having his secretary (attorney was out-of-town) work with father's attorney to finally have father return the children at the library. Mother lost two hours of her first weekend with all three children due to father trying to control the exchange point. He only agreed to this temporarily until the next court hearing.

Although this case is ongoing, remember your support system is there for you to connect with to vent your feelings. They back you up on your return communications. Because you know his game so well, you will see it and refuse to play. Initially, be prepared for him to come at you harder or attack you. Just remain focused and stick with the facts. Know that his game may continue until your children age out of the court system or even beyond. By keeping this in mind, you can avoid being blind-sided by his communications, behaviors, or attitudes.

Keep a level head and let him continue to be the person he is while getting on with your life. It is important that he not disrupt your normal life rhythm. This means you are moving on even if he remains stuck in his unhealthy patterns of behavior and communication.

Reality Check #6 **Control Freak Co-Parents and You**

Learning to co-parent with a coercive controller is another skill you are developing. Most of us do not come pre-programmed knowing how to co-parent with a coercive controller because this is not a relationship we anticipate having. We have to learn the skills to negotiate with someone who has motives focused on maintaining power and control.

There are parents who are able to communicate and agree to maintain similar parenting styles with their children. These are parents who easily fit into what the courts expect from co-parents. However, when parents are constantly in conflict, it becomes difficult to maintain this co-parent relationship. In these cases, it is better for the children and their parents to use a parallel parenting model.

Parallel parenting is where you determine your rules and family structure in your home and let go of your ex parenting in the same way you do. This allows you to devote your energy to being the kind of parent you want to be without being controlled by the other parent. Your children benefit because you are nurturing and attentive to them while letting your ex decide how he wants to parent the children when he is responsible for them.

In order to co-parent or parallel parent with a coercive controller, you have to understand what makes the particular coercive controller tick. Then, you have to identify the particular patterns of the coercive controller. This is important so you are not lured into his net again.

Each chapter of this book that explains the attitudes, behaviors, and belief systems of the particular coercive control tactic includes an assessment to help you figure out the pattern. Then, you are guided through two types of Focus Points™. The first type of Focus Points™ help you clearly understand the exact process the coercive controller uses with you. These are followed by Focus Points™ to help you determine what course of action you choose to take to avoid being pulled back into his net.

Coercive Control Tactics in Co-Parenting

The coercive control tactics that are most commonly seen in co-parenting disputes include the areas originally identified as power and control behaviors. Additionally, three tactics specific to Family Court are identified. These types of coercive control tactics help you look for how your ex may be using uninformed individuals working on your divorce or custody case to continue to abuse you.

These tactics include: (1) Using emotional abuse;(2)using male privilege; (3) using children; (4) using minimization, denial, and blaming; (5) using economic abuse; (6) using intimidation; (7) using threats and coercion; (8) using isolation; (9) using spiritual abuse; (10) using litigation abuse; (11) using court-appointed professionals; and (12) using family court judges; (13) using nonphysical sexual abuse; (14) using physical abuse/violence, even after separation or divorce; (15) using physical sexual abuse. It is important for you to understand clearly what each of these tactics are in order to identify the patterns used in your relationship. Then, you can communicate clearly with Family Court professionals.

They are explained below.

Coercive Control Tactics

Coercive control tactics are patterns of behavior designed to maintain power and control over a partner or children in a relationship. These patterns of behavior can happen without any physical contact with the victim. Physical abuse and physical sexual abuse are also patterns of coercive control tactics that require direct physical contact with the victim. These are all considered forms of interpersonal violence.

When an abuser repeatedly uses various coercive control tactics, the victim develops the ability to predict the outcome of the abuser's behavior. An abuser will not necessarily engage in all types of coercive control tactics with a victim. Rather, the abuser may selectively use several tactics to maintain power and control over his victim. If the victim successfully leaves the relationship and separates from the abuser, the abuser may resort to other coercive control tactics in an effort to regain dominance over the victim.

After a separation or divorce, the abuser may manipulate other adults involved with the victim to carry out his coercive control tactics with her. The abuser is very skilled at using coercive control tactics. The abuser may inadvertently manipulate court-related professionals and judges who are uninformed about these patterns. Without realizing it, they are carrying out his desires for power and control over his former partner.

I must strongly emphasize the importance for everyone to understand the nature of coercive control tactics. In addition, family members, your support system, and professionals must know how an abuser manifests them. This knowledge can help family members, your support system, and professionals avoid being unintentionally pulled into manipulative behaviors and becoming a proxy abuser for your former partner.

As a quick review, here is a diagram of the types of coercive control used by abusers. You can come back to this whenever you want to identify the type of coercive control tactics being used against you.

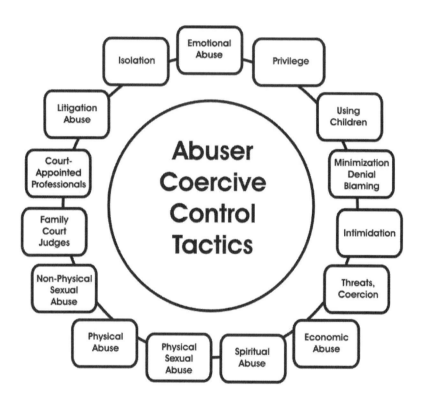

Each tactic is described briefly below. You can skip directly to the chapter in the book to learn more about how the abuser uses the tactic and ways you can stop the tactic from being used against you.

Types of Coercive Control Tactics, Briefly Described

Here are some brief definitions of the types of coercive control tactics. For more in-depth descriptions, please refer to the chapter for each coercive control tactic. This guide will help you find the chapters in Section II that fit your situation more quickly.

The Leopard Who Constantly Changes His Spots (Using Emotional Abuse) is any kind of abuse that attacks the other person without physical contact. Emotional abuse involves anything from verbal abuse and constant criticism to more subtle tactics, such as repeated disapproval or the refusal to be pleased about anything about the other person. It is a constant wearing down of self-esteem, self-confidence, sense of self-worth, or sense of identity. While there is no physical contact, there is still the sense of being hit internally. This may be a feeling of heartache, stomachache, or even feeling beaten down. Emotional abuse attacks the person through all of their senses.

The Lion King of my Castle Co-Parent (Using Male Privilege) is attitudes and behaviors representative of a male-dominated patriarchy. Males who use this tactic are motivated by the belief that they are superior to you; they have all the answers for you; and know what is best for you and your children. They assert this attitude through their behavior, and if that does not work, escalating coercion to force you to do their bidding. Their underlying motivation is control.

The Sneaky Snake Co-Parent (Using the Children) is when an abuser has the attitude his children are his property. He places his needs, wants, and desires above those of his children even to the point of using them as pawns to get back at or take revenge on their mother. He is not concerned about how his attitudes and behaviors affect his children.

<u>The Wolf in Sheep's Clothing Co-Parent</u> (Using Minimization, Denial, and Blaming) "Minimization" is when the abuser denies the seriousness of his coercive control tactics and criticizes you for having an emotional response to his actions. The abuser downplays the impact of his behaviors and actions. For example, he may claim you are "too sensitive" or "cannot take a joke." He will tell you "it was not as bad as you are making it sound."

"Denial" is when the abuser acts as if he would never do anything wrong, hurtful, or mean. He acts confused when you tell him you are hurt or scared by his behaviors. He may claim "you are making way too much of a small situation." His comments may be something like "it was not that bad, the bruise will heal, or you will get over it."

The abuser uses "Blaming" to say you are the reason he behaves in hurtful, spiteful, or angry ways. He tells you "you are responsible for the way he acts toward you." Or he may say "you caused him to hurt you emotionally or physically." He refuses to accept any responsibility for his words or behaviors.

<u>The Pompous Hog Co-Parent</u> (Using Economic/Financial Abuse) involves controlling the money to get you to do what he wants. He may do this to keep you from becoming economically and financially independent to care for yourself and your children. The abuser may take your money, refuse to give you money for necessities, or have you beg him for money to buy something special you want. He may damage your good credit while maintaining his good credit or pull you down with him financially.

<u>The Intimidating Badger Co-Parent</u> (Using Intimidation) is attitudes and behaviors used to raise fear of harm at the hands of the abuser. Intimidation is used to gain power over you and manipulate you to respond as the abuser desires even if this is counter to your desires. You are often caught in a Catch-22 with

the abuser when you attempt to comply with his demands because he changes his demands so you can never respond correctly.

The Threatening Skunk Co-Parent (Using Threats and Coercion) are attitudes and behaviors used to force you into doing what the abuser demands under threat of loss of something or someone special to you or threat of bodily injury. These attitudes and behaviors are used to gain power over you and force you to respond to the abuser's desires without question. The problem is the consequences may be life-threatening or lead to death. Threats and coercion are used to escalate your fear of the abuser beyond intimidation.

The Laughing Hyena Co-Parent (Using Isolation) involves attitudes and behaviors designed to restrict your movements and maintain physical and emotional control of you. The abuser is focused on detaching you from contact or communication with anyone who is supportive or involved in your life. The purpose of isolation is to monopolize your attention and keep you occupied with only receiving information and input from him. It is a way to keep you from having other supportive people in your life.

The Prickly Porcupine Co-Parent (Using Spiritual Abuse) means keeping you from practicing your religion or spiritual beliefs. The abuser criticizes or makes fun of your religious or spiritual beliefs, background, or practices. He refuses to allow you to practice your beliefs in your home when you are together. He refuses to allow you to share your religious and spiritual beliefs with your children. He wants to dictate what you can and cannot teach your children after divorce. He misquotes or uses religious writings to his advantage regarding the relationship between men and women. He may mock your faith, sabotage or limit your faith practices, and misuse religious texts to justify his abusive actions or demands.

Court-related Coercive Control Tactics

The following three types of coercive control tactics are specific to any type of legal involvement with the Family Court. They may occur whether there are children from the relationship or not. While some Family Court professionals are gradually understanding and learning about coercive control tactics, there are many individuals involved in this system who remain uninformed. These types of coercive control are discussed in Section III of this book.

The Slippery Weasel Co-Parent (Using Litigation Abuse) is use of all parts of the Family Court legal system to delay, extend, control, and coerce you into going along with his demands. Litigation abuse may be used to punish you or take revenge on you for leaving him. He may use this type of abuse to keep you from telling about the amount and types of his coercive controlling or abusive behaviors during the relationship. The abuser may send you tons of legal paperwork after you leave. He may continue to talk to you with words on paper when he no longer is able to speak to you directly so he can lecture you or tell you what you need to do or think.

The Lying Rat Co-Parent (Using Court-Appointed Professionals) means bringing in experts to address custody/parenting issues. His purpose is to criticize and undermine your parenting skills that were okay before you separated. The abuser uses court-appointed professionals to show he is a "good enough" parent and to have you held to a higher parenting standard than he is expected to show.

The Charging Rhinoceros Co-Parent (Using Family Court Judges) is the abuser's way to prove to the court his lies about his former partner. It is his way to project his own behaviors onto his former partner. His purpose is to make his former partner look as if she is trying to get in the way of his parenting relationship with the children. He is trying to prove to the court that he is the stable, responsible parent. The purpose of his behavior could be to get back at or hurt his former partner for leaving. He may want access to the children so he can begin or continue to abuse them.

Physical and Sexual Coercive Control or Violence

While many uninformed individuals only consider physical and sexual violence as domestic violence, as you have seen to this point, there are many other types of coercive control originally called domestic violence. I have taken the liberty to address these three areas last because too many members of society as well as professionals fail to recognize the most subtle and insidious forms of domestic violence.

Many years of research demonstrates that physical and sexual violence, as means of power and control, often follow years of coercive control. These forms of coercive control may be the abuser's last resort when all the previous types of coercive control tactics have failed. Therefore, it is important to include them, as they may be the ultimate reason for leaving the relationship or marriage. It is important for you to make this distinction when speaking with Family Court professionals and judges.

The Stalking Fox Co-parent (Using Non-Physical Sexual Abuse) as coercive control is attitudes and behaviors that imply you are his property, and you are tied to him in a relationship, even if you are divorced. The coercive controller sends these types of messages by sliding comments into communications about who, when, where, and how you can have intimate relationships.

This may come across as statements that he does not like who you are seeing because you are exposing "his" children to someone he does not like. He may threaten to take the children away from you if you say you are getting married or your new partner is moving in with you. He may say, "I don't want another guy raising my kids." His goal is to undermine any relationship you may develop that is supportive of you. The implication is that you are and always will be his property even if he decides to marry again. Therefore, you are never to marry again.

The Chest Beating Gorilla Co-Parent (Using Physical Abuse) is "an act carried out with the intention, or perceived intention, of causing physical pain or injury to another person" (Straus & Gelles, 1986). This is behavior intended, at a minimum, to cause temporary physical pain to the victim. It includes relatively "minor" physical actions like slapping with an open hand up to severe acts of violence that lead to injury and/or death. It may occur just once or sporadically and infrequently in a relationship, but in many relationships it is repetitive and chronic, and it escalates in frequency and severity over time.

The Territorial Tiger Co-Parent (Using Physical Sexual Abuse) involves attitudes and behaviors that are motivated by the abuser's feelings of entitlement and rights to be physically sexual with their partner or spouse whenever, however, and wherever they feel like it. Sometimes abusers show sexual respect to their committed relationship partner prior to marriage.

Sometimes, it is only after marriage abusers engage in sexual coercion and abuse. In an abuser's mind, sex is now his right and he is entitled to sex because he has a certificate of marriage. His interpretation of this certificate is that he now owns you, and your choices are no longer his concern.

Each coercive control tactic summarized above is described in more detail in the next sections of this book.

Reality Check #7 **Set Strong Boundaries with Control Freaks**

Coercive controllers are boundary violators. They are only interested in themselves. They will violate boundaries of their spouse/partner, their children, other family members, friends, and acquaintances. In order to understand more fully the boundaries they violate, it is important to understand what your boundaries are.

Boundaries are related to your personal physical space, your emotional space, and your spiritual space. Your personal physical space helps you determine how, when, why, where, what, and who may touch your body or come close to you physically. It plays a role in whether you feel comfortable or violated around different people. You have the right to protect your physical boundaries from being violated. This means if you say "take your hands off me" that means right now! If you say "don't touch me" that means keep your hands or other body parts from making contact with my body.

Any type of unwanted touch or getting too close to you is a violation of your physical boundaries. In different cultures, there are different distances between people that are considered comfortable and safe, and distances that are uncomfortable. For most Americans, this translates to 18 inches in front of a person and about two feet on either side or behind a person.

Here is an exercise to help you test your physical boundaries. Pair up with someone you do not know well and stand about six feet apart. Slowly walk toward each other until one of you starts to feel uncomfortable. The person who feels uncomfortable first should signal for both of you to stop. Stop right where you are. Ask someone else to measure how far apart you are standing. How close is it to 18 inches?

Next, stand still while the other person goes behind you and stands about six feet away. Have the person who is six feet away start to walk toward you until you turn your head to see how close they are. This is the signal for the walker to stop. Measure the distance. It will probably be about two feet.

Finally, ask the walker to stand about six feet to the side of you. Have the walker start toward you until you turn your head to see where they are. The walker stops and the distance is measured. It will probably be about two feet. With this exercise, you have defined your personal physical space.

Now, what do you do when there is not enough room for you to stand within your personal space? This can happen in many situations. You could be in an elevator, in a line at the grocery store (although if you look, you will see the cart helps keep that 18-inch to two-foot distance), or moving through a crowd. Then, you automatically watch who is around you and protect your body as others around you are doing the same. Try this out the next time you are in this situation.

Besides your physical boundary, you also have a physical/sexual boundary. Your physical/sexual boundary helps you determine who, when, where, how, and why someone can touch you sexually. When you were starting to go through puberty, you may have experienced boys making unwanted sexual advances. This may have been in the form of brushing up against you in hallways or classrooms, making comments about your body developing sexual parts, or sitting too close and touching you in a sexual way.

These are all violations of your physical/sexual boundaries. You have a right to stop someone from touching you in a way that has sexual overtones. You can do this by saying, for example: "back off and stop trying to touch me," "remove your hand from my leg, arm, or around my shoulders," "don't hug me," or any other similar statement. You have a right to guard your personal boundaries in this way with every other person, including your intimate partner, spouse, or former spouse. If you do not desire sexual contact, you have the right to say "stop that right now." We will discuss later how coercive controllers use non-physical sexual comments as a means of sexually abusing you.

Emotional boundaries protect your right to be respected around your thoughts, feelings, and opinions. Remember, your thoughts are your understanding about the world and how it works for you. What you think about and know is important to you. You have a right to think your own thoughts.

Your feelings are your experience of the world through your five senses. They are neither right nor wrong, good nor bad. They are personal to you and based on your present and past experiences. You have a right to feel your own feelings.

Your opinions are based on your life experience and are expressions of what you have come to understand through your own thought processes. They may be the same or different from another person's opinions. They are neither right nor wrong, good nor bad. They are your opinions based on your life experience, your acquired knowledge, and your personal judgments. Your opinions belong to you, and you have a right to have them.

Your spiritual boundaries are your belief system. They are acquired through your religious education, your experience of how you believe the world works, and how you interact with the world at large. There are many forms of organized religion as well as other spiritual paths available for humans to explore. There is no one right path. It is what works for you. You have a right to choose your own spiritual belief system.

We all have boundaries in each of these areas. You have the right to set your boundaries for what works for you. You also have the right to live your life based on your physical, physical/sexual, emotional, and spiritual boundaries. No one has the right to tell you how to live in these areas unless you are violating laws or taking advantage of others. The same is true for coercive controllers. They have no right to violate your sacred boundaries.

How do you maintain your sacred boundaries with a coercive controller? You refuse to allow the coercive controller to violate your boundaries. You confront the coercive controller on boundary violations if you think it is safe to do so. You can stop the coercive controller from violating your boundaries by refusing to engage on an emotional level with him. Through this book, you will learn how to set and maintain your personal boundaries.

Other types of boundary violations abusers use include monitoring/surveillance, stalking, violence against children, abducting children, and threats of litigation. These boundary violations keep you constantly on edge, watching for his next unexpected appearance or attempting to figure out how to protect your children from abuse, neglect, or kidnapping.

Your life is not your own because you are caught up in his constant interference in your life. When you get support from an advocate or well-informed therapist about this type of behavior, it is easier for you to move forward and make a life of your choosing. This is important for your mental and emotional health and for bringing this level of health to your children.

Transformational Journaling™ Techniques

Earlier, I provided background on how Transformational Journaling™ developed. To review, Transformational Journaling™ is a 3-step process. First, you will look back at where you have been in your life. Second, you look at where you are today on your journey. Finally, you make conscious choices about where you want to go from here. You will use Focus Points™ to help you work through these three steps.

How to do Transformational Journaling™

Step one: In your journal, describe in as much detail as possible the specific coercive control tactic pattern the abuser used in your relationship (refer to the diagram in Reality Check #3 as a quick reference). The more you are able to be specific, the easier it will be for you to see if he continues to use that pattern after you are separated/divorced.

Step two: Determine the boundary you want to set about his use of the coercive control tactic pattern.

Step three: Write out, in as much detail as possible, how you want to address his use of that pattern in your parallel or co-parenting communications. Be cautious about how you plan to do this so you keep yourself and your children safe.

Step four: Talk with a safe friend, advisor, or counselor about what you plan to say to make sure you stay focused on your intention and leave out any emotional hooks that can trigger a negative response from the abuser.

Section II

Control Freak Tactics
Know your Voice

In the following sections of the book, you have an opportunity to identify the coercive control tactics your abuser uses. Most importantly, you want to look for repeated patterns of coercive control tactics. When you are able to identify the coercive control tactic patterns, you can share them with people in your life who fail to understand your experience. In this way, you find your voice to speak your truth about what has happened in the past and what may be happening in the present.

Reality Check #8 **The Constantly Changing His Spots Leopard Co-Parent (Using Emotional Abuse)**

Overview of the coercive control tactic pattern—Using Emotional Abuse

Using Emotional Abuse is any kind of abuse that attacks the other person emotionally or mentally without any physical contact. Emotional abuse involves any type of verbal abuse and constant criticism to more subtle tactics, such as, repeated disapproval or even the refusal to be pleased about anything about the other person. It is a constant wearing down of self-esteem, self-confidence, sense of self-worth or sense of identity. While there is no physical contact, there is still the sense of being hit internally. This may be a feeling of heartache, stomachache, or even feeling beaten down. Emotional abuse attacks the person through all of their senses.

Case examples of the coercive control tactic pattern—Using Emotional Abuse

How do you explain to someone who has not experienced emotional abuse what happens in your relationship? This was the question one protective mother asked me after expressing her frustration that her attorney did not understand what she was saying when she told him she was emotionally abused in her relationship. Here's where her communication was unclear and what the attorney failed to ask to clarify what she was saying. She lumped all the abuse she experienced in her relationship under the label "emotional abuse" because she did not realize the abuse she experienced also involved other kinds of abuse.

Her attorney interpreted what she was saying through his limited understanding of abuse and boiled it down to "he yelled" at her a few times and maybe "called her names" a couple of times. And, there were a couple of times he "threatened to kill her" if she left. Because her attorney viewed the abuse as a few isolated incidents and failed to recognize the abuse as a pervasive pattern in the relationship, he dismissed her concerns as not important to parenting time decisions.

When I interviewed this mother to find out how I could support her through her divorce process, I asked her specific questions that helped me understand what coercive control tactics her husband used in the relationship. She told me he would order her around, insist that cleaning the bathroom daily was more important than spending quality time with the children, and that she should awaken at the early hour he woke up to go to work and get the children up at the same time. He never recognized any of the important nurturing activities she did with the children, the importance of reading before bedtime, or making decisions about how things happened in the home.

Nothing she wanted to discuss was important to her husband, while anything he wanted to discuss always came first. He never complimented her, but was quick to criticize her. She explained an example of this when it came to food she prepared for dinner. She prepared nourishing healthy meals that took into account her digestive health problems. These meals were not what he was accustomed to and he often complained that there was not enough food to eat even when there was more than enough for the entire family. He insulted her by going to his mother's home and getting food that his mother prepared and bringing it back home to eat in front of his wife. Then, he compared his wife's "insufficient" meals to the better meals his mother cooked.

Her husband did not view these methods of emotional abuse as hurtful. He refused to acknowledge that he was insulting his wife for her beliefs about the health and wellness of her family. His demanding and coercive controlling behaviors left her feeling diminished and lacking as a wife and mother. He portrayed himself as the one who was "always right" and she was "always wrong." She felt emotionally beaten down by his words and behaviors and lost trust in her own judgment.

When we went through the assessments in this book, this woman was able to clearly identify the different forms of emotional abuse she experienced. She was, also, able to identify other coercive control tactic patterns used toward her in the marriage. She learned to communicate clearly with her attorney and court-appointed professionals, and clarify her testimony in court.

This is just the first of a series of assessments for you to review as you go through this book. You will easily recognize some of the patterns identified in the assessments, and you will see that other patterns were not present in your relationship. As you consider each item, think about the coercive control tactics that were present in your relationship and how you would describe them to someone who is unfamiliar with coercive control or domestic violence.

This will help you communicate clearly with attorneys, court-appointed personnel, judges, and mental health therapists as well as other professionals who have little or no understanding of coercive control tactics.

Now, it is time for you to begin your assessment of your relationship while you were together and after your separation. If you prefer to print out the assessments so you can circle your responses, go to HouseOfPeacePubs.com to respond to the assessments. You will use what you discover with your Focus Points™.

The directions for this and all the assessments are the same. I will give the directions before each assessment of the coercive control tactic in your relationship.

Using Emotional Abuse

1 __never, 2 __hardly ever, 3 __sometimes, 4 __often, 5 __quite often, 6 __not applicable, 7 __prefer not to answer

Column 1 = In the relationship; Column 2 = After you separated/divorced

In the relationship	After you separated/ divorced	Emotional Abuse
1 2 3 4 5 6 7	1 2 3 4 5 6 7	1. Your ex used rituals of degradation with you.[2]
1 2 3 4 5 6 7	1 2 3 4 5 6 7	2. Your ex performed unannounced room searches.[2]
1 2 3 4 5 6 7	1 2 3 4 5 6 7	3. Your ex forced confessions from you.[2]
1 2 3 4 5 6 7	1 2 3 4 5 6 7	4. Your ex forced you into lockdowns (where you are not permitted to leave your room or the house or use the phone for a period of time).[2]
1 2 3 4 5 6 7	1 2 3 4 5 6 7	5. Your ex used periods of forced silence.[2]
1 2 3 4 5 6 7	1 2 3 4 5 6 7	6. Your ex denied you access to rights of personal hygiene, eating, sleeping, and/or toileting.[2]

1 2 **3 4 5 6 7**	1 2 3 4 5 6 7	7. Your ex suppressed conflict and resistance.[2]
1 2 **3 4 5 6 7**	1 2 3 4 5 6 7	8. Your ex created and enforced rules for everyday conduct.[2]
1 2 **3 4 5 6 7**	1 2 3 4 5 6 7	9. Your ex used information shared by you of terrorizing, humiliating, or abusive childhood experiences as reenactments.[2]
1 2 **3 4 5 6 7**	1 2 3 4 5 6 7	10. Your ex called you names, yelled at you, and/or refused to listen to anything you wanted to say.[5]
1 2 **3 4 5 6 7**	1 2 3 4 5 6 7	11. Your ex forced you to violate your religious beliefs.[51]
1 2 **3 4 5 6 7**	1 2 3 4 5 6 7	12. Your ex trained you to react in predetermined ways to cues, such as finger snapping, a set number of telephone rings, a nod, two taps of the foot.[2]
1 2 **3 4 5 6 7**	1 2 3 4 5 6 7	13. Your ex insisted he set the terms for every encounter: if you tried to walk away from an argument or refused to get out of bed in the middle of the night to review your faults or tried to sit separate, you were reminded that the lecture, interrogation, sex, job, or "the relationship ends when I say it ends."[2]
1 2 **3 4 5 6 7**	1 2 3 4 5 6 7	14. Your ex demonstrated the ultimate expression of property rights: the right of disposal illustrated by the statement frequently preceding Femicide (female murder): "If I can't have you, no one will."[2]
1 2 **3 4 5 6 7**	1 2 3 4 5 6 7	15. Your ex caused the sudden destruction or unexplained disappearance of familiar objects that had special meaning to you.[2]

1 2 3 4 5 6 7	1 2 3 4 5 6 7	16. You sometimes wonder, "What's wrong with me? I shouldn't feel so bad."[52]
1 2 3 4 5 6 7	1 2 3 4 5 6 7	17. You frequently feel perplexed and frustrated by your ex's responses because you can't get him to understand your intentions.[52]
1 2 3 4 5 6 7	1 2 3 4 5 6 7	18. Your ex seems to take the opposite view from you on almost everything you mention, and his view is not qualified by "I think" or "I believe" or "I feel"--as if your view were wrong and his were right.[52]
1 2 3 4 5 6 7	1 2 3 4 5 6 7	19. Your ex is either angry or has "no idea of what you are talking about" when you try to discuss an issue with him.[52]
1 2 3 4 5 6 7	1 2 3 4 5 6 7	20. You sometimes wonder if your ex sees you as a separate person.[52]
1 2 3 4 5 6 7	1 2 3 4 5 6 7	21. Your ex seems irritated or angry with you several times a week or more although you did not mean to upset him. You are surprised each time. (He says he is not mad when you ask him what he is mad about, or he tells you in some way that it's your fault.).[52]
1 2 3 4 5 6 7	1 2 3 4 5 6 7	22. Your ex engaged in "gaslighting." For example, he deliberately gave you false information with the intent of making you doubt your own memory, perception, and sanity. Instances may range simply from the denial by your ex that previous abusive incidents ever occurred, up to the staging of bizarre events by your ex with the intention of disorienting you.[53]

1 2 3 4 5 6 7	1 2 3 4 5 6 7	23. Your ex rarely, if ever, seems to want to share his thoughts or plans with you.[52]
1 2 3 4 5 6 7	1 2 3 4 5 6 7	24. When you felt hurt and tried to discuss your upset feelings with your ex, you didn't feel as if the issue was fully resolved, so you didn't feel happy and relieved, nor did you have a feeling that you've "kissed and made up." (He says, "You're just trying to start an argument!" or in some other way expresses his refusal to discuss the situation.).[52]
1 2 3 4 5 6 7	1 2 3 4 5 6 7	25. You cannot recall saying to your ex, "Cut it out!" or "Stop it!"[52]
1 2 3 4 5 6 7	1 2 3 4 5 6 7	26. You are upset not so much about concrete issues--how much time to spend with each other, where to go on vacation, etc.--as about the communication in the relationship: what he thinks you said and what you heard him say.[52]

How does he do that?

Your ex may have a way to indicate to you that anything you say has no value and what he says carries the only value in the relationship. He can do this in many ways, such as, ignoring anything you say as if it is not important, or finding something wrong with what you say. His goal is to shut you up so that you lose your voice to speak your mind or express your knowledge or opinions.

This is a very subtle way of removing your identify and self-worth. You begin to doubt yourself and start asking for his suggestions about everything in your life. You leave all the decisions to him and do whatever he says. When you finally decide to leave, you experience a sense of loss about who you are.

This destruction of your identity and self-esteem may come across to attorneys and other professionals as you being a weak and unempowered person. Initially, you may agree that is how you feel; however, as you retrieve what has been hidden inside you, you start to stand up for yourself, what you know, what you believe, and who you truly are as a human being.

This may throw your attorney, court professionals, and ex off-guard because you are changing before their eyes. Your domestic violence advocate is supportive of you stepping into your own power. However, your ex increases his control through his attorney and court professionals to attempt to "put you in your place." Stay strong and remember you are empowered to be yourself. No other human being has a right to control you.

Another way your ex may have controlled you emotionally is through looks or gestures that left you feeling powerless. These looks and gestures will be attempted in different settings as you go through the divorce and ensuing custody process. It is important to remember that these nonverbal cues arise from his lack of physical access to you. Ask your attorney to stand in court in a way to block your view of him, or ask for separate rooms for mediation.

Over time, you will stop noticing these gestures and looks because you know your ex is only trying to use them to control you. You have moved beyond his ability to control you. You will respond from an empowered position that will result in him stopping his behaviors because they no longer have any effect on you.

Use your Transformational Journaling™ Focus Points™ to clearly identify the emotionally abusive patterns your ex used in your relationship. Then, determine how you choose to respond in the future.

How to respond to the coercive control tactic—Using Emotional Abuse

Start your Focus Point™ process here with the first question.

Focus Point™: What patterns do you see that are similar between what happened while you were in the relationship and what is happening since you left the relationship?

Next, look at what new patterns your ex may be doing since you left the relationship.

Focus Point™: What new patterns do you see your ex using since he does not have direct physical access to you?

Now, take the third step and look at how your ex uses emotional abuse in his co-parenting responsibilities.

Focus Point™: How is your ex using the patterns as a co-parent?

These Focus Points™ are for journaling by you on how to approach the abusive parent in the future related to the specific coercive control tactic "Using Emotional Abuse."

Focus Point™: Identify where in your life your ex is able to trigger you to respond to his demands just as he did in your relationship.

This Focus Point™ is the crucial piece to help you move on with your life and avoid getting caught in the coercive control traps your ex may be using. Take some time to envision your life as you want it to be. You may find talking this over with other protective mothers can help you define a life free from abuse in all your relationships.

Focus Point™: Determine how you want to set up healthy

boundaries to protect yourself in the future from being abused through "Using Emotional Abuse."

Examples of how other protective parents approach an abusive parent with the specific coercive control tactic pattern—Using Emotional Abuse

One mother I work with was continually getting emotionally abusive e-mails and text messages from her ex. She would get caught in the emotional abuse and immediately start defending herself. This would escalate his return e-mails to her, which included constant threats of taking her back to court for violating the court order.

With some support, I was able to show her what he was doing and how she was pulled into the emotionally abusive relationship with him again. We started labeling his coercive control tactics until she could identify his patterns. From there, we reworked her e-mail responses so that there was nothing her ex could grab onto to escalate the issue. She saw very clearly his pattern of always having to have the last word or e-mail. Therefore, once the issue was resolved, she stopped responding so that he would stop baiting her.

Now, the majority of the time, this protective mother responds to e-mails from her ex without getting caught up in the emotional abuse he is using. However, she knows that it is still easy for him to trigger her. Before she replies to any of his e-mails, she asks me to review what she wants to send to help her take out anything that would escalate him.

How does this take care of her feelings she wants to express? She talks those feelings over with me and actually is heard. This is something he will never do. She sees the humor in how easy it is to still get caught up in the abusive cycle and appreciates being able to choose a different path.

The long-term outcome is that the e-mails from her ex are less abusive because he does not gain the benefits of getting into a fight with her. She maintains a better co-parent relationship with him because she no longer believes she has to please him or comply with his demands. Thus, this protective mother has become a parallel parent with her ex and he is free to parent as he chooses. Their children are learning to work with different types of people in authority and building resiliency skills for life. It works for everyone in the family.

Debra A. Wingfield, Ed.D.

Reality Check #9 **The Lion King of the Castle Co-Parent (Using Male Privilege)**

Overview of the coercive control tactic pattern—Using Male Privilege

Using Male Privilege is defined as attitudes and behaviors that represent a male-dominated patriarchy. Males who use this tactic are motivated by the belief that they are superior to women; they have all the answers for women; and know what is best for their wives and their children. They maintain this attitude through their behavior, which is motivated by control. If their coercive behavior does not work, they escalate coercion to force a woman to do their bidding. This attitude may best be explained by patriarchal comments, such as: "A man's home is his castle"; "I can do whatever I want in my own home, and law enforcement (society) cannot tell me what I can and can't do."

Male privilege also includes the attitude that the man is omnipotent (meaning he is God) in his home. This is expressed by statements like, "It's my way or the highway"; "You'll do whatever I tell you without protest, disagreement, or refusal"; "I brought you into this world, and I can take you out"; "You better do as I say or else...".

Outside the family in dealing with societal sanctions, the abuser uses the "Good ole boy" network to play up to other men, asking them to be in agreement with him. His attitude may come through in comments like: "You just have to put a woman in her place"; "She may say 'no' to sex, but she really wants it."

Case examples of the coercive control tactic pattern—Using Male Privilege

One coercive control tactic (and the first one mentioned in the assessment below) involves the abuser's use of a "letter of instruction." This may take different forms. The abuser may present you with a daily "To Do" list that you must account for at the end of the day. If you fail to follow the list or miss something on the list, the usual consequence is some form of abuse. The abuse may be verbal, emotional, or physical.

A variation on the letter of instruction may come to you after you separate or divorce. This may be an e-mail, text message, or a physical letter given to you by your child or mailed through the post office. The letter is written to tell you what you may or may not do with your child, what you are expected to do if your child needs to have an appointment arranged, or how your ex has arranged an appointment to meet his schedule.

Another form of the letter of instruction is an e-mail that attacks you for doing something that your ex believes you did just to hurt him. He may use threats, intimidation, or coercion to get you to comply with his way of doing things. If you chose not to do things according to his wishes, he sees this as grounds for going back to court to take away some of your time or privileges with your children.

You may feel emotionally beaten up by your ex after he uses this method of instructing you. When you are in court and attempt to tell the judge what you were wanting to do for your children, the judge may cut you off and take your former partner's side. If this happens more than once, you may decide it is better to comply with the abuser's instructions so you do not get dragged back into court repeatedly, where the judge may conclude you are not making a strong effort to co-parent. This could result in you being placed on supervised visits with your children or sent to "alienation therapy" for you to learn how to encourage your children to see their father even if that is not their desire.

In my work with protective mothers, I have seen judges side with the abuser and punish the mother even if the abuser's requests are unreasonable and not in the best interests of the children. When this happens, I help protective mothers find a balance between challenging everything the abuser requests and making choices that help them protect their children. Through the use of Transformational Journaling™ techniques, you will learn and gain the skills I teach protective mothers.

Before we get to your assessment, let us look at another example of how abusers use male privilege before and after separation. Your ex may have shown extreme jealousy when you were together. He may have expressed this by letting you know that you were not to look at, talk to, or have any contact with men other than him.

If you and your ex went to a party and one of the male guests approached you to start a conversation, you may have received a certain look or gesture from your ex that told you walk away or you would pay for it later. Paying for it later may have involved various types of abuse that could include an all-night lecture, the silent treatment, or a beating.

After you separated or divorced, your ex would still expect that you would not have a relationship with another man. If you did, he would see this as a betrayal of your relationship with him because he still views you as his property. Therefore, you would receive messages directly from him or indirectly through the children that he did not like who you were with and did not want this new man in your life parenting his children.

If you decide to remarry, he may see this as a reason to take you back to court and demand sole custody of the children. He may relocate to remove the children so you can no longer have any parenting time with them. He could go so far as to prevent the children from talking with you by phone and might refuse to bring them for supervised visits, which you would still have to pay for since the visiting time was already arranged. This is his way of punishing you for moving on with your life.

The punishment your ex uses on you may become even more extreme if you have a child or children with your new husband. He may brainwash your children against you and teach them to think you are a bad woman who does not deserve them in your life. He may tell your children mean and nasty things about their half-sisters or brothers that will discourage them from wanting to have a relationship with their half-siblings. His goal is to cut you off completely from any relationship you may have had with your children prior to your divorce or his gaining sole custody.

By the time your children reach adulthood, you will have to wait for your children to reach out to you to form a relationship. This takes time and may bring up unresolved emotions from the past and stress for you. When this does occur, I recommend you find a competent professional therapist, knowledgeable about coercive control tactics, who can help all of you gradually reunite.

This process requires healing for you and your children. Be patient with your children as they separate truth from fiction, and keep the focus on developing your relationship with them. Their relationship with their father is none of your business, and it is best to leave that out of the conversation.

You can use your Transformational Journaling™ techniques to help you while you are in the process of healing your parent-child relationship. If your children are interested in sorting through their issues with Transformational Journaling™ techniques, check out *Through a Child's Voice: Transformational Journaling™* at HouseOfPeacePubs.com click on the products link , a book I wrote especially for this purpose. Your qualified therapist can help you find the best way to share your discoveries made in your journaling process.

Assessment of the coercive control tactic pattern—Using Male Privilege

Now, it is time for you to begin your assessment of your relationship while you were together and after your separation. If you prefer to print out the assessments so you can circle your responses, go to HouseOfPeacePubs.com and click on the Interpersonal Violence Assessments link to respond to the assessments. You will use what you discover with your Focus Points™.

Using Privilege

1 __never, 2 __hardly ever, 3 __sometimes, 4 __often, 5 __quite often, 6 __not applicable, 7 __prefer not to answer

In the relationship	After you separated/ divorced	Using Male Privilege
1 2 3 4 5 6 7	1 2 3 4 5 6 7	1. Your ex made all the decisions in the relationship, regardless of knowledge or skill.[2]

1 2 3 4 5 6 7	1 2 3 4 5 6 7	2. Your ex and males in the family expected and received higher quality goods and services.[2,6] For example, fathers and sons received higher quality and more food and clothing; more seating that is comfortable, beds, more privacy, better and longer sleep.
1 2 3 4 5 6 7	1 2 3 4 5 6 7	3. Your ex formalized his rules by writing them down.[2,6] For example, he wrote "Instructions" for spending money, sexual relations, raising children, or other aspects of the relationship.
1 2 3 4 5 6 7	1 2 3 4 5 6 7	4. Your ex made you agree not to make him jealous.[2]
1 2 3 4 5 6 7	1 2 3 4 5 6 7	5. Your ex made and enforced rules regarding your behavior without your input.[2,6] For example, he told you, "If you do not answer within 30 seconds after I ask you a question and I have to ask you again, be prepared to pay for it." [2]
1 2 3 4 5 6 7	1 2 3 4 5 6 7	6. Your ex required you to use a log book and record everything you did during the day, followed by questioning you nightly to find fault, and beat you regardless of what you did or wrote down.[2]
1 2 3 4 5 6 7	1 2 3 4 5 6 7	7. Your ex refused to allow outsiders to get involved in the relationship.[2] For example, suggestions from others about how to treat his partner are ignored or met with hostility; you were blamed if outside persons offer to help or interfere with his "property rights."
1 2 3 4 5 6 7	1 2 3 4 5 6 7	8. Your ex believed and behaved as if he had "property rights" concerning you or your daughters.[8] For example, he verbally, sexually, emotionally and/or physically abused "his" women merely because they were female.

1 2 3 4 5 6 7	1 2 3 4 5 6 7	9. Your ex interfered with you developing relationships with other men after you separated, even though he developed a new relationship that lead to marriage.[5]
1 2 3 4 5 6 7	1 2 3 4 5 6 7	10. Your ex encouraged sons to use their "special male status" in the home.[8] For example, sons have higher status, greater privileges, and more freedom than daughters do; sons are allowed to verbally, emotionally, physically, or sexually abuse their mother or sisters.
1 2 3 4 5 6 7	1 2 3 4 5 6 7	11. Wives and daughters (regardless of age) in the family are expected to wait on husbands, fathers, and sons.[8]
1 2 3 4 5 6 7	1 2 3 4 5 6 7	12. If you work outside the home, you worked a "second shift" when you got home.[2, 6] For example, you did all of the cooking, shopping, cleaning and childcare before and after you "went to work." His workday was finished once he arrived home from work. [8]
1 2 3 4 5 6 7	1 2 3 4 5 6 7	13. Your ex told you that he is more important than anyone else in the family because he is male.[2, 6] Your ex supervised you and your work as if you were an employee.[2, 6] For example, he told you, "The bedspread must be exactly one and 3/8 inches off the floor;"[2] you must vacuum daily, "so you can always see the lines";[2] your "work performance" was often judged and criticized.
1 2 3 4 5 6 7	1 2 3 4 5 6 7	15. Your ex believed he had a right to use you sexually when and how he wanted.[2, 6] For example, "If I decide that we sleep together, you will humbly comply without a fight;" "Do not physically resist me;" "Don't make me ask you three times."[2]

1 2 3 4 5 6 7	1 2 3 4 5 6 7	16. Male partners and males in the family received more nurturing, support, and attention than female partners and daughters.[8] For example, males received more encouragement to do well in school or at work, more tending when they were sick, and more focus on their lives and interests
1 2 3 4 5 6 7	1 2 3 4 5 6 7	17. Your ex claimed you as his private property, to do with as he pleases. Property rights were signed on paper or symbolically claimed, for example, by burning or tattooing your arm to let other men know you belong to him;[2] by "loaning" you or your services to other men; by replacing you; or by otherwise "throwing you away" when he's finished with you.

How does he do that?

Have you ever received a "Letter of instruction" from your coercive controlling partner or similar verbal instructions? At first, you may have taken this as something your partner was attempting to use to communicate with you effectively when he was not present. If this is your first committed relationship or first marriage, you may think this is normal communication between partners. However, it is important for you to understand that partners do not provide specific instructions for their partner.

In a healthy relationship, if a list is needed to communicate or plan for the future, partners are likely to develop the list together. Occasionally, if one partner will be gone from home for a period of time, he or she may provide the other partner with a list of items for caring for the home, their own needs, or handling certain personal matters for them. You may put together a list so that your partner can follow through when you are away from home as well.

This is different from the kinds of lists that a coercive controller may generate. A coercive controller may give his partner a list providing specific instructions that she must follow.

How to respond to the coercive control tactic—Using Male Privilege

It is important to understand that this tactic violates your boundaries in the area of sexism. Sexism is about saying one gender is superior to the other. Therefore, if a male sees himself as superior to you because he "is a man," then this is a huge red flag that tells you to run as fast as you can away from him.

Sexism may be expressed in words, such as, "I am the provider and I know what is best for my family," or "It is my job to take care of my family to make sure they have a house to live in, food on the table, and clothes to wear" or "Any needs beyond the basics are the responsibility of my wife." As I write this, I see all kinds of problems with statements like this.

First, there is a message of ownership with the use of the word "my." Second, the stereotype of the man making the money and providing for the material needs of the family is outdated. Third, the message that the woman's role is to care for, nurture, and meet the emotional needs of the family is also outdated. All of these stereotypes are designed to keep women at home looking for the man to provide for her while he goes out and conquers the beast of the outside world.

Today, women hold more than 50% of all jobs. They are a major part of the workforce and contribute equally to society in their work. The problem occurs when men expect women to help meet the financial needs of the home, plus perform all the stereotypical women's roles at home: shopping for groceries, preparing meals, caring for children, maintaining a clean home, and nurturing and guiding children to adulthood. Many abusive men still see their role with their children as strictly a disciplinarian. They fail to understand the importance of daily interaction and nurturing children as an important quality in child development.

This supports their sexist attitude and belief system that supports their stance of using male privilege. Their unrealistic expectations come out in terms of the attitude that they own all members of the family; sexual rights to their wife, and at times, sexual rights to their daughters and sometimes sons. In addition, their attitudes toward children's behavior can lead to excessive physical punishment that may be abusive.

In domestic violence groups with court-ordered abusers, I found some men refuse to allow their sons to lose a fight and force their sons to go back and finish the fight until they win. Teaching violence to their sons is just a step away from teaching their sons that they have to win all fights with their wives no matter how much violence is needed to make it happen. They lack empathy skills to understand the impact of their demands on their wives or children.

Now, it is time for you to take a careful, open-minded look at how your ex "Used Male Privilege" in your relationship. Go back and review the assessment again to look at how your ex used Male Privilege during your relationship and how your ex may still be "Using Male Privilege" in your co-parenting relationship. You will use your journal to describe in detail how your ex used the patterns with you during your relationship and how these tactics are still being used against you.

Start your Focus Point™ process here with the first question.

Focus Point™: What patterns do you see that are similar between what happened while you were in the relationship and what is happening since you left the relationship?

Next, look at what new patterns your ex may be doing since you left the relationship.

Focus Point™: What new patterns do you see your ex using since he does not have direct physical access to you?

Now, take the third step and look at how your ex Uses Male Privilege in his co-parenting responsibilities.

Focus Point™: How is your ex using the patterns as a co-parent?

This Focus Point™ is for your journaling on how to approach the abusive parent in the future related to the specific coercive control tactic "Using Male Privilege."

Focus Point™: Identify where in your life your ex is able to trigger you to respond to his demands just as he did in your relationship.

This Focus Point™ is the crucial piece to help you move on with your life and avoid getting caught in the coercive control traps your ex may be using. Take some time to envision your life as you want it to be. You may find talking this over with other protective mothers can help you define a life free from abuse in all your relationships.

Focus Point™: Determine how you want to set up healthy boundaries to protect yourself in the future from being abused through "Using Male Privilege."

Examples of how other protective parents approach an abusive parent with the specific coercive control tactic pattern—Using male privilege

In my work with protective mothers, I discovered their ex's attempt to "Use Male Privilege" would often send them on an emotional roller-coaster. This feeling of spinning out-of-control lead to responses that continued to give their ex-partner/spouse control over them.

In order to break this cycle, I encouraged them to write out exactly what they wanted to say to their ex as a venting process. Once they vented, they would share this with me (usually via e-mail). Together, we would review what they wrote and I would validate their feelings about their partner's use of the coercive control tactic. Then, we would rewrite the e-mail, staying closely focused on what the facts were they needed to respond to and leaving out all their feelings. Then they would send this rewritten version of the e-mail to their ex.

This was how these protective mothers set up boundaries with their ex. There was no emotional engagement by the protective mothers with their abusive ex. Therefore, there was no longer a way to get into a win-lose situation with the abuser. Over time, the abusive partners stopped trying to snare their former female partner into a fight because it did not work.

The next ploy from the abusive ex is often an attempt to be nice and appear to cooperate. This is often a manipulative tactic to pull the protective parent back into the power and control game. At this stage, the protective mother would continue to share her potential responses with me to avoid being drawn back into the abuser's net. She would then communicate with her ex in a straightforward way, without emotion and without making any triggering statements. This form of straightforward communication eventually leads the abusive ex to communicate in the same way because he no longer receives any emotional benefits from creating a fight.

The other advantage to only using straightforward communication is your abusive ex will not gain any ammunition to take you back to court. If you do not write any emotionally laden e-mails, he cannot use those kind of e-mails to prove to the court you are unstable. Abusive co-parents actually make themselves look bad if their e-mails are out-of-bounds and accusatory when yours are factual, concise, and non-emotional. This can save you a lot of trauma and drama, and you avoid hours of anxiety about how he is treating you.

Specifically, from a "male privilege" standpoint, he is no longer able to hook you into his sexist attitudes. You see right through what he is doing and just continue to move forward with your life on your terms. He is left to face his life and the consequences of his own behaviors.

Reality Check #10: **The Sneaky Snake Co-Parent (Using Children)**

Overview of the coercive control tactic pattern—Using the Children

"Using the Children" as a coercive control tactic with his partner is defined as attitudes and behaviors that provide the abuser with permission to objectify their children and give him ownership of them. An abuser develops the attitude his children are his property. He places his needs, wants, and desires above those of his children, even to the point of using them as pawns to get back at or take revenge on their mother. He shows no concern or empathy for the impact of his attitudes and behaviors on the lives, growth, socio-emotional and physical development of his children. He is unaware of the impact of his attitudes and behaviors on his children.

Case examples of the coercive control tactic pattern—Using Children

Brainwashing children against their protective mother is a common coercive control tactic used before and after separation or divorce. The motivation behind this tactic is to break the bond between the mother and her children. Underlying this motivation is jealousy that the mother has a special relationship with her children that is different from the father-child relationship.

The father does not understand that his relationship with his children is different from their relationship with their mother, and that this difference is normal. What he sees instead is a closeness that he yearns to have with his children that they have with their mother. Because of his controlling behaviors, the children may not trust him in the same way they trust their mother. This fuels his jealousy. He fails to realize his attitudes and behaviors result in the strain in his relationships with his children.

Therefore, he shifts to a place of coercive control with his children to force them to have a relationship with him. It appears to be a win-lose situation for him because he may take it to the extreme of completely cutting the children off from their mother. When these children reach adulthood, most of them reach out to their mother and disengage from their father. Thus, it is truly a lose-lose situation for him.

This tactic can take many different forms. He may "Use Litigation Abuse" to accuse the mother of parental alienation and say the children either don't want to be with him or they don't want to talk with him while they are with their mother. This cognitive distortion (thinking error) is of his own making because he does not support the children having a positive relationship with their mother.

If he succeeds in court and is supported by custody evaluators, the Guardian ad litem (GAL), or other court-appointed personnel, the mother may end up with various inappropriate sanctions. These may include therapy by a court-involved therapist to teach the mother how to not alienate the child, mother may only be able to have supervised visits for a very limited time each week or month, or outright threats on the mother's life that may lead to her fleeing the area.

All of these sanctions are forms of "Financial Abuse" and "Intimidation", "Threats and Coercion" tactics being carried out in his name by the court. The harm to the children can be lifelong because it causes mental anguish and physical disengagement from the protective parent. When the adult children reach out to reunify with their protective parent, they do not know how to express the anguish and pain they feel about their separation. The parent they want to know does not necessarily know how to reunify with her own children.

The means to start this reunification process may depend on the ages the children were when they were taken (kidnapped is the language many parents use because it feels the same way). If the relationship with the child was interrupted at a young age, before the child was five or six years old, there is an initial stage of getting to know their mother.

In one case, the child was separated from the mother from age 15 months to 21 months. He completely forgot who his mother was and needed to gradually be re-introduced to her. This separation at a crucial developmental point resulted in angry behavior from the child and even at age three, he struggled with his feelings of trust and safety. The long-term impacts of this separation from his primary caretaker can result in major psychological and neurodevelopmental problems later in life.

For children who are separated at an early age and not reunited until they are adults, it can take several years for their relationship with their protective mother to develop into a secure, trusting one. This relationship may have many power struggles as mother wants to pour out her love to her child that was locked up over all the years of separation. The child may initially feel smothered by mother's outpouring of love and attention.

It is helpful to build this relationship with an adult child as you would build a relationship with another adult. The difference is a biological connection that is not as strong as the emotional connection and desire to reunite. Create new traditions with your adult children and allow them to set the pace for developing the relationship as well as the boundaries for your relationship with them. This is a respectful way to reunite after years of separation and possible brainwashing.

Brainwashing is one coercive control tactic abusers use to interfere with the mother-child relationship. Abusive fathers may use consistent negative comments about the mother with their children. Some of the name-calling and verbal bashing he used directed toward the mother while in relationship with her is continued with the children. He may not have direct contact with the mother, but he can paint the mother in negative terms that the children then repeat to the mother.

This may lead the child to direct verbal attacks toward the mother or to question her: "Why does daddy always say ___ about you?" Ultimately, this coercive tactic backfires on the abusive father because the children know in their heart that these words are not true. Often, these children start rejecting the father and grow closer to their mother.

Fathers often take this response from their children as mother is trying to get them away from him, and he then accuses her of doing exactly what he has been doing. Untrained court personnel, professionals, and judges may not understand that the problem is the behavior of the father, not the mother. The father paints the picture in court that he is being estranged from his children and blames his ex for doing this.

The court tends to see this type of testimony as the opposite of what it is. The court is likely to grant the father more parenting time with the children. This is just one example of how courts contribute to damaging healthy relationships between mothers and children.

Assessment of the coercive control tactic pattern—Using Children

Now, it is time for you to begin your assessment of your relationship while you were together and after your separation. If you prefer to print out the assessments so you can circle your responses, go to HouseOfPeacePubs.com and click on the Interpersonal Violence Assessments link to respond to the assessments. You will use what you discover with your Focus Points™.

Using Children

1 __never, 2 __hardly ever, 3 __sometimes, 4 __often, 5 __quite often, 6 __not applicable, 7 __prefer not to answer

In the relationship	After you separated/ divorced	Using Children
1 2 3 4 5 6 7	1 2 3 4 5 6 7	1. Your ex hurt or allowed others to hurt your children. [2]
1 2 3 4 5 6 7	1 2 3 4 5 6 7	2. Your ex told the children in front of you, "If your mother isn't here when you come home from school, look under the ground in the backyard, right where the dog is buried." [2]
1 2 3 4 5 6 7	1 2 3 4 5 6 7	3. Your ex threatened to take the children or took the children and refused to let you see them after he gained primary physical and legal custody. [5, 6] For example, he interfered with your parenting time after gaining primary or sole parenting of your children.
1 2 3 4 5 6 7	1 2 3 4 5 6 7	4. Your ex used your children to give messages to you.[5]

1 2 3 4 5 6 7	1 2 3 4 5 6 7	5. Your ex used visitation as a way to harass you.[5]
1 2 3 4 5 6 7	1 2 3 4 5 6 7	6. Your ex made statements that led you to feel guilty about the children.[5]
1 2 3 4 5 6 7	1 2 3 4 5 6 7	7. After gaining custody, your ex refused to let you see the children for one year or more, then let you see the child now and then for a day at a time – if you were very grateful and never demanded your children back. He dictated terms of parenting time you would have with your children.[5, 6]
1 2 3 4 5 6 7	1 2 3 4 5 6 7	8. After your ex won custody, he moved away without entering the court system or without telling the court of his intention to move, or he moved away and permanently kidnapped the children.[6]
1 2 3 4 5 6 7	1 2 3 4 5 6 7	9. After you separated, your ex sought unapproved contact with the children or kept you from having contact. For example, he kidnapped the children, kept the children longer than allowed, and/or returned the children to you later than allowed.[4]
1 2 3 4 5 6 7	1 2 3 4 5 6 7	10. Your ex undermined your parenting.[7]
1 2 3 4 5 6 7	1 2 3 4 5 6 7	11. After you separated, your ex became extremely attentive to your children after having minimal involvement while you were married or in your relationship.[6]
1 2 3 4 5 6 7	1 2 3 4 5 6 7	12. Your ex convinced your children that you did not love them because you slept with someone else.[6]
1 2 3 4 5 6 7	1 2 3 4 5 6 7	13. Your ex threatened to tell authorities that you are a lesbian or gay, strung out on drugs, or mentally unstable so they will take the children.[6]
1 2 3 4 5 6 7	1 2 3 4 5 6 7	14. Your ex engaged in brainwashing your children against you. [4, 6] For example, he constantly bad-mouthed you until the children began to believe him.

1 2 3 4 5 6 7	1 2 3 4 5 6 7	15. When you were given custody of your children, your ex relinquished parental rights to avoid paying child support. Only after your children were adults did your ex attempt to develop a relationship with them.[5]
1 2 3 4 5 6 7	1 2 3 4 5 6 7	16. Your ex threatened to take the children "any time" he hears you are "misbehaving" (as in having an affair).[6]
1 2 3 4 5 6 7	1 2 3 4 5 6 7	17. Your ex left your children alone for weeks with a caretaker, but refused to allow you parenting time when he was unavailable to care for your children.[6]
1 2 3 4 5 6 7	1 2 3 4 5 6 7	18. You lost custody of your children at young ages and they were raised by your ex mother-in-law or another caregiver.[5, 6] For example, after getting custody, your ex turned over primary care of your children to another person, such as his new wife, a live-in girlfriend, or other caregiver.[4]
1 2 3 4 5 6 7	1 2 3 4 5 6 7	19. Your ex made sure your visitation/ parenting time was limited to a few hours each week.[6]
1 2 3 4 5 6 7	1 2 3 4 5 6 7	20. Whenever your child said she/he wanted to live with you, she/he were not allowed to see you.[6]
1 2 3 4 5 6 7	1 2 3 4 5 6 7	21. Your children are not allowed to talk about you with your ex, tell you they love you, or smile when they talk with you by phone.[5]
1 2 3 4 5 6 7	1 2 3 4 5 6 7	22. Your children were told to tell you what they wanted before a court hearing by your ex because it was what your ex wanted them to say.[5]
1 2 3 4 5 6 7	1 2 3 4 5 6 7	23. When you decided to move out, your ex physically prevented you from taking the children.[6]
1 2 3 4 5 6 7	1 2 3 4 5 6 7	24. Your ex insisted on joint custody as a strategy to reduce his child or spousal support payments.[5]

1 2 3 4 5 6 7	1 2 3 4 5 6 7	25. Your ex led the children to believe that their safety depended on remaining close with him.[5]
1 2 3 4 5 6 7	1 2 3 4 5 6 7	26. Your ex used child custody court as a way to control you.[6] For example, you were threatened to lose your children if you did not give your ex primary legal and physical custody. You were threatened with a custody battle if you did not agree to the parenting agreement written by your ex.[5]
1 2 3 4 5 6 7	1 2 3 4 5 6 7	27. Your ex monitored your phone calls, e-mails, text messages, or video calls with your children so they did not feel comfortable sharing with you during that time.[5, 6]
1 2 3 4 5 6 7	1 2 3 4 5 6 7	28. Your ex coached, bribed, or pressured the children to lie about you in court.[5]
1 2 3 4 5 6 7	1 2 3 4 5 6 7	29. Your ex blamed the divorce or separation on you; made sure the children knew that the spiritual and emotional costs to everyone in the family were your fault.[5] For example, he showed the children extreme religious texts or videos stating that divorce is a sin, and that sinners go to hell; taught children that women's role is to keep the family together, no matter what.[5]
1 2 3 4 5 6 7	1 2 3 4 5 6 7	30. Your ex would alternate kindness and abusiveness with the children to create a trauma-induced bond with the children.[5]
1 2 3 4 5 6 7	1 2 3 4 5 6 7	31. Your ex questioned the children about visits as a way to gather information about you.[5] For example, he demanded to know, in detail, what they did, who they visited, where they went, who they saw, what they drove.
1 2 3 4 5 6 7	1 2 3 4 5 6 7	32. Your ex made the children believe that anything you do for them is done only to make *him* look bad.[5]

1 2 3 4 5 6 7	1 2 3 4 5 6 7	33. When you were given custody of your children, your ex never tried to talk to them, or write, call, or send cards or gifts.[5, 6]
1 2 3 4 5 6 7	1 2 3 4 5 6 7	34. After gaining primary parenting time with your children, your ex failed to give you enough advance notice of special events in your children's lives so you could attend.[5]
1 2 3 4 5 6 7	1 2 3 4 5 6 7	35. When you had your ex's baby after you separated, he refused to accept the child as his saying, "That is not my child because I don't make boys or girls" or other comments denying the possibility of paternity.[5]

How does he do that?

An abuser may use a wide variety of coercive control tactics related to his children. After reviewing all of the tactics in the assessment above, you may feel overwhelmed. My suggestion is that you pick out the tactics most often used and describe them so you are very clear as to what the patterns are and how he repeats those patterns over time.

Focus Point[TM]: My ex "Uses the Children" in the following ways:

1.

2.

3.

4.

5.

Consider how your coercive controlling ex "uses the children" as a means to continue to control you. He may do this in very subtle ways so you do not catch onto what he is doing until later that day or even the next day. On the other hand, he may be right up front and tell you what you have to do in order to keep seeing the children or be involved with them. Remember, his goal, whether conscious or not, is to keep you off-balance and doing what he wishes.

Some of the subtle ways your ex can keep you off-balance is to undermine your parenting. If you and your child come up with a solution to a problem your child is having, and your child wants to implement the solution in both homes, your ex may sabotage your efforts by preventing your child from using that solution in his home. This is his way of saying you cannot control anything that happens in his home or with your child in his home. In fact, I often find the abusive ex will do exactly the opposite in his home.

Let us take an example of this type of coercive control tactic. If your child is taking advantage of their cell phone usage while in your home, you decide to restrict use of the phone to certain hours of the day or put the phone off-limits during certain activities, such as, no phone use during meal times. You want your child to learn to respect meal times as a family time where phone calls are either not answered or the person calling is told they will have to be called back.

Your ex decides you are being too demanding by requiring your child show respect to you and other family members during meal times. He allows your child to accept phone calls during meals because then he is free to ignore your child. He is subtly teaching your child to disrespect him as well as you. When your child reaches adulthood, he or she will disrespect friends, co-workers, and intimate partners. This leads the child to see themselves as the center of attention and always expecting to get his or her way.

Whether he realizes it or not, this coercive controller attitude is teaching the child narcissistic behaviors.

There are seemingly countless ways coercive controllers use children. If we go through the list (in the assessment) of ways coercive controllers use children, we could identify many more examples of how abusers use children to control a co-parent. Instead, it will be more helpful for you at this point to take the five coercive control tactics you identified and describe in detail how the abuser uses your children to indirectly control you.

Focus Point^{TM}: Take each tactic you identified in the previous Focus Point^{TM} and describe in as much detail as possible how your abusive ex "Uses the Children" to coercively control you. Hint: You may find it easier to complete this Focus Point^{TM} in your journal or in a separate notebook.

How to respond to the coercive control tactic–Using the Children

When your ex "uses your children" as a means to coercively control you, this often leads to your most highly charged emotional reactions. I want to respond to your emotional reactions as well as how you help your children handle this type of abuse by their father. For children, this is often the most confusing type of coercive control used against you because they receive double-bind messages (messages that make them wrong no matter how they respond). These messages make it difficult to separate what is directed toward you and what is directed toward the children. We will discuss how you respond effectively to your ex and to your children.

First, let us talk about your response to the coercive control tactics your ex uses when he is attempting to control you through your children. For the most part, in the early months after separation, many protective mothers feel overwhelmed with emotion about every part of leaving an abusive and controlling relationship. This is a normal reaction, and once you understand this, it helps you settle down and focus on the issues.

Give yourself permission to have your emotional reactions to issues. This is an important part of the process of healing. Use your journal or notebook to vent. Get all your feelings out in writing so they are no longer running around in your head. We call this squirrel cage thinking. You have to get your head cleared so you can think clearly. If there are some emotional points you want to come back to later, you have them written down and you can highlight them for future reference.

From my experience and the experience of many other protective mothers, I find "squirrel cage thinking" often hits about 2:00 a.m. when you are least likely to call your best friend. Get those thoughts out of your head and on paper (in your journal) so you can go back to sleep. You have all those thoughts about scripts you are writing to say exactly what you want to say to him, what you wished you said to him, or what you are going to say to him to review in the light of day. Are you chuckling yet?

After you actually get some sleep, you can wake up and, with a clear head, decide what you choose to keep and what you now see as something you would never say. Circle what you want to keep and disregard the rest. You may want to expand on what you want to keep or reword it to be a very straightforward, fact-based message. Now, call your best friend and share what you wrote and what you decided you would do. Take any helpful feedback and revise your response one more time. Make sure you are now focused only on facts and your emotions are no longer in the message.

This keeps you focused on your co-parenting responsibilities and avoids attempting to fix your ex because you cannot fix him. He is not going to change or try to be the kind of father you wish your children had. He will still be the same coercive controller you tried to build a relationship with before you recognized the warning signs. Your goal and focus now is on protecting your children and yourself from further abuse.

Now that you are calmed down, focused on the issues, and prepared to communicate effectively with your ex, it is time to work with your children. Children of all ages know who is a safe parent and who is unsafe. They have great intuition and will save their emotional work to do and questions for the safe parent. This means you get the full range of emotions from them. They will be happy, joyful, and share all their good situations with you. They will also be mad, angry, and may lash out with the rage they have built up when they are with their abusive father.

Although it is unfair for you to have to handle all the negative emotions, remember your children feel safe with you to let those emotions out. You can teach them effective ways to express those emotions so they don't hurt themselves, you, or anyone else. Their emotions and questions often come during transition times. For example, after you pick your children up from a visit with your ex, you greet them and then get quiet or prompt them to talk about whatever is on their minds.

When your children share their thoughts and feelings, you may feel a strong need to respond by solving problems they share or correcting misinformation. Instead, just listen and let them talk. This is their way of venting. If they ask a question, answer it as simply as possible and then get quiet. If there is another question, let them bring it up. If you have questions, you can always go back to the issue later and remind them of the conversation. Let your child know you were thinking about their statement or question, and ask if they are willing to talk about it.

By simply listening, you give your children space to get comfortable with you again after a time apart. This is especially important if the abusive parent monitors their contacts with you closely. They need this reconnection time to shift their minds to the different rules in your home and the different ways that communication occurs. Children talk in metaphors and ask questions that may be on their minds for some time. If they have something else they want to talk about related to the specific subject, they will circle back around to it later.

Now, the most important issue I find puzzles most protective mothers is how to build the skills their children need to set healthy boundaries with their abusive father. These skills include physical, emotional, and sexual boundaries. Let us define each type of boundary in this context, and then we will talk about the skills to set and maintain those boundaries.

Physical boundaries involve any type of contact with a child's body by the abusive father or anyone else. Any type of contact with the child that results in bruises, marks, or pain is a boundary violation. It is crucial that you teach your children that any type of hitting, pushing, shoving, spanking that leaves marks (I personally don't believe in spanking, but I know some parents think this is okay.), grabbing a child by their arm, their ear, or their hair, or other physical touch that causes the child pain is outside acceptable boundaries. The child needs to be empowered to report this type of behavior to a responsible adult who has the authority to take action to protect them.

Emotional abuse is much harder for children to understand and it is difficult for them to set boundaries around what feels bad to them. Children do understand when something does not feel right inside their body because someone said something hurtful or talked about them to someone else in hurtful ways. Some of this now is taught in bullying prevention programs. Talking with your children about how to identify emotional abuse is an important way you can support this type of education in the school, and helps you protect your children when they are with their abusive father. Find out what the bullying prevention education program is teaching and use this as a stepping-stone to help your children understand emotional abuse. Remember what Robert Fulghum said, "sticks and stones may break *(y)*our bones, but words can break *(y)*our hearts."

To help your children learn to protect themselves from emotional and verbal abuse, teach them that they can say, "It hurts my heart when you talk to me like that." If they are unable to be assertive about how words are hurting them, teach them they can picture the words bouncing off their bodies because they have a special glass bubble that surrounds and protects them.

This is a visualization I use with children and adults to help them create this picture in their minds. Imagine yourself inside a glass bubble where you can see and hear everything around you. The glass bubble allows you to let kind and nurturing words come into you where you can bring them into your heart. If someone says something to you that is hurtful to you or about someone else, you can let those words bounce off the bubble and fall to the ground.

Sexual abuse includes any type of grooming behaviors as well as actual physical sexual contact with children. Sometimes children who are placed with an abusive father were being groomed to accept physical sexual contact prior to separation. When the protective mother attempts to prevent the abusive coercive controller from having unsupervised parenting time with the children, this can backfire. Sometimes the courts actually give sexually abusive coercive controllers sole parenting time and sole decision making authority, with the protective mother only allowed supervised visits.

Help protect your children from sexual abuse by letting them know they can share anything they want to with you. Teach them that that their bodies are private. Once they reach a point where they can bathe, dress, and care for their hygiene issues alone, they should be allowed total privacy in this area of their lives. By the time children are seven years old, they want privacy to take care of themselves. Empower your children to expect this from you and from their father.

Find out if your child's school is teaching children about "Good Touch, Bad Touch" or using similar programs that teach children about sexual abuse. These programs can help you empower your child to protect himself or herself from sexual abuse by a parent, primary caregiver, coach, or other adult. Most sexual abuse occurs between a child and someone the child knows. Help your children feel comfortable in talking with you about sex and anything that happens they don't like or makes them feel uncomfortable.

Children can be taught to go to teachers, school principals, counselors, or to dial 911 and talk to law enforcement if they are being physically hurt, feel emotionally unsafe, or are being sexually hurt. They can come to you with their concerns or let you know this is happening to them if it is safe to do so. Sadly, we have learned when children go to their protective mother with these issues and the protective mother subsequently reports the abuse to Child Protective Services, the mothers often are blamed for the abuse rather than believed.

Use caution if reporting abuse by the coercive controlling co-parent because it is more difficult to protect your child if contact is cut off from you. These are tough decisions to make. We will discuss them in more detail in the monthly Q & A calls available to you. Learn more about these calls at HouseOfPeacePubs.com and click on the AskDrDebraW link. Focus Points™ are for journaling by you on how to approach your abusive co-parent in the future related to the specific coercive control tactic-—Using the Children.

Focus Point™: What "Using the Children" coercive control tactics do you see that are similar between what happened while you were in the relationship

Now, take some time to reflect on how your ex is currently behaving toward you. What is new? What are the same old behaviors, words, and actions used, just on different topics?

Focus Point™: What new patterns do you see your ex using with your children since he does not have direct physical access to you?

What behaviors, words, and actions is your ex using around co-parent issues? What is the same as during your relationship? What is different since you separated?

Focus Point™: How is your ex using the pattern "Using the Children" as a co-parent?

Now, look at your triggers your ex learned about you while you were in the relationship. Your triggers may be around protecting your children physically, emotionally, sexually, or from neglect. These triggers may be how your parenting was undermined or how he took advantage of special gifts you gave your children that lead to his jealousy. There are many triggers or buttons your ex learned to push while you were in your relationship. How are those still being used against you? Then, identify how he is still using those triggers.

Focus Point™: Identify where in your life your ex is able to trigger you to respond to his demands on issues with your children just as he did in your relationship.

Next, take some time to establish your boundaries so your ex is no longer able to abuse you through his use of the children. His communication with you should be free of comments about your choice of lifestyle or your standards of care for your children. He should refrain from manipulating the children, brainwashing them with lies or insinuations about you, or preventing them from being able to talk with you without supervising their communications.

Remember, your children need to be kept out of any responsibilities for giving you messages, carrying notes or child support payments, or in any way carrying out the terms of your divorce agreement. If the pattern is currently established, you can change that by alerting your ex that this is harmful to the children and an alternative must be found.

As you write on this Focus Point™, keep some of these boundaries in mind and any other boundary violations you identified in the assessment in this chapter.

Focus Point™: Determine how you want to set up healthy boundaries to protect yourself in the future from being abused through "Using the Children."

Examples of other protective parent's approaches to an abusive parent with the specific coercive control tactic pattern—Using the Children

One of the areas that protective mothers find disturbing is how coercive controlling co-parents attempt to put their children in the middle to carry messages between the parents. He tells the children to remind their mother of something or just to pass this message onto their mother. Children put in this situation are very upset by this type of request because they often forget part of the message or do not give the message as it was given to them. Adults put in this situation as children talk about how they disliked this happening to them.

How do you stop this type of behavior? First, you need to vent your emotions with your safe person about how this hurts your children. You have many tools to do this and the Transformational Journaling™ Focus Points™ provided here walk you through that process.

Another tool you can use is talking to a supportive friend who can listen and validate your feelings. You have a right to express your feelings as you experience them. However, if you express your feelings to a coercive controller, you may find them twisted and used against you. I know you are familiar with this behavior. It may be one reason you left the relationship. Therefore, you want to identify someone who can help you sort out your feelings from the facts. You will find that just focusing on the facts when communicating with a coercive controller does not provide an opening for him to attack you.

One protective mother told me learning this two-step skill allowed her to start healing, keeps her grounded, and keeps her focused on what is important. She said, "It works!" She does this by writing an e-mail to vent that she sends to me. We talk about her feelings and her frustration with her ex. Then, we decide what facts she needs to communicate to him. She then sends this revised e-mail to him.

If the coercive controller in your life is using the children to relay messages to you, your e-mail or text may state that you received the following message from your children and you want to clarify the message as received. Then, you say that it would be much easier and more helpful to both of you as you co-parent to communicate directly, instead of through your children. That way the message does not require clarification.

Since many methods of communication are available, there is no reason for you or your ex to involve the children to carry messages back and forth. Find what works best for both of you. Keep using that communication method until your ex realizes this is how to get a response from you. You are modifying his behavior and that takes time. For example, you keep your responses focused on the facts related to the communication. You ignore the baiting to get you emotionally upset. Your ex learns over time that you will no longer be baited and stops or seldom uses baiting language in his communications. No matter what the issue is between you and your co-parent, use these same steps to resolve issues and stop building ammunition for him to use in court.

If he does take you to court, you have a written record of what occurred between the two of you. This important documentation tells the court you are attempting to work with him for the "Best Interests of your Children." Fact-based documentation should be the focus of court consideration and not emotional testimony or lies and twisted information. If the court does not allow you to testify about everything in your records, you can ask to have the e-mails or text messages admitted into evidence to support your appeal.

Another example of coercive control using the children is taking advantage of the protective mother on a care-taking basis. There are several variations on this type of abuse. First, father asks mother to take the children during his parenting time because he is going out of town for work or vacation. Then, he expects mother to give up part of her parenting time to stay within the number of days per year the children are with each parent.

A little different twist on this is to ask mother to keep the children and then not offering to give her additional money for her expenses. Another way he plays this is he does not give mother any notice that he is leaving town, even though he knew ahead of time, and expects she will change her plans to accommodate him.

A reverse of this situation is that father will ask someone in his family to take care of the children when mother has already told him she would prefer the children are with her when he is out of town. An additional way this works is he takes the children while mother is out of town, but refuses to give up his normal schedule to switch with mother, so the children are with him for an extended period of time beyond the spirit of the court order.

You may have a different variation of this situation. You may or may not receive additional financial support from father. You may have to reveal more about your plans than you want to in order to gain his agreement to care for the children. You may end up finding an alternative if he refuses to cooperate. Notice that through all these variations he is controlling the outcome. You are expected to bend to his wishes while he is free to select what he wants to do.

Some protective mothers find their coercive controlling ex attempts to remove the children from contact with her. He may do this through lies and false allegations in court. He may obtain sole physical and legal custody/parenting time, and then refuse to allow her visits or parenting time as stated in the court order. He may go so far as to request that she have supervised visits, and the court may grant his request. These supervised visits may make it difficult for you to manage if you do not have the money to pay for the visits.

If this happens, you have to decide what strategies you want to take to remedy this situation. There are many options and resources to consider. Some mothers found that they were drained emotionally and financially from all the court drama. They took some time to find themselves first before finding other means to maintain contact with their children. This is not to say they abandoned their children to the coercive controller. These mothers realized that getting back in touch with their confidence and competence put them in a better place to return to court and demonstrate their ability to care for their children.

Remember, your children are resilient and they will recover from being shut out of your life. It may take some time for them to reach out to you after they turn 18 and age out of the court system. Your children know you are their mother and they have an important bond with you that will tug them back to you in time. It is your responsibility to be ready for them and to support their needs at that time.

Adult children will let you know what they need from you. They may have questions about why you left, how you left, and why they ended up with their father. Be honest and share the truth with them. If there are court papers that will answer their questions, make sure you

provide those papers with any lies or false allegations noted. Many court orders contain fabricated information or misinformation written by a judge who is judging you, not the facts. Help your children learn the facts. Let them make their own judgments.

Allow your relationship with your adult children to develop slowly and on their terms. There may be a lot of brainwashing you have to wade through to help them get an accurate picture of who you are. The best way to teach your children who you are is to be you. Show them your inner strength, your confidence, your competencies, and most of all your unconditional love for them. They will relate to you as best they can.

If your adult children find themselves in psychotherapy or mental health counseling, encourage their involvement and become involved if they request it. Follow the guidance above to share with them the truth and give it to them in small amounts so they can digest it. This is a long process for their recovery from living with a coercive controller and finding out who you really are, not a distorted view presented to them by their father. Allow healing to happen in its own time.

Debra A. Wingfield, Ed.D.

Reality Check # 11   **The Wolf in Sheep's Clothing Co-Parent (Using Minimization, Denial, and Blaming)**

Overview of the coercive control tactic pattern—Using Minimization, Denial, and Blaming

Using Minimization, Denial, and Blaming is refusal to take responsibility for any coercive control tactics. The abuser makes light of his attitudes and behaviors and projects his responsibility onto the victim. He implies she is too sensitive, says she cannot take a joke, and discounts the emotional and physical pain she experiences.

With minimization, the abuser who is in denial discounts the victim's responses. The abuser shows irresponsibility and lack of empathy for the impact of his attitudes and behaviors on the victim and/or the children. He feels justified in his attitudes and behaviors because he presents himself as knowing that he would never do anything wrong, hurtful, or mean.

The abuser uses blaming to place all the responsibility on the victim. He says, in essence, this is why he behaves in a hurtful, spiteful, angry, or violent way toward her. Basically, he says, "It is all her fault, she made me do _____," thereby, absolving himself of any responsibility.

111

Case examples of the coercive control tactic pattern-Using Minimization, Denial, and Blaming

One father told me that it was not his fault that he pushed his wife out of the car during an argument. He said "she told me she wanted to get out of the car because she was sick of the fighting" so I reached over her, opened the door and pushed her out. While he admitted to pushing her out, he blamed her for his behavior because she said that was what she wanted him to do.

He, also, neglected to mention that he was traveling at about 30 MPH when he pushed his wife out of the vehicle. This level of minimization fails to acknowledge that she could have been seriously hurt or had life-threatening injuries. Although the children were not present during this incident, it could have easily happened with the children in the car.

In another case, the father had a history of getting drunk and driving. One evening, on their way to a family dinner, the mother asked the father to stop the car and let her drive because of his drunkenness. He refused. When he stopped for a red light, she instructed the daughter to get out of the car as she opened her door to leave the car. This drastic measure caused the father to allow his wife to take over the driving. Then, he minimized the danger to her and their daughter while she drove to the family dinner. His wife decided from that point on that she would meet him with their daughter for family dinners rather than have him do the driving.

This type of minimization and blaming with the added denial of him causing danger to his wife and child as well as himself is very common.

Now, it is time for you to begin your assessment of minimization, denying, and blaming in your relationship while you were together and after your separation. If you prefer to print out the assessments so you can circle your responses, go to HouseOfPeacePubs.com and click on the Interpersonal Violence Assessments link to respond to the assessments. You will use what you discover with your Focus Points™.

Using Minimization, Denial, and Blaming

1 __never, 2 __hardly ever, 3 __sometimes, 4 __often, 5 __quite often, 6 __not applicable, 7__prefer not to answer

In the relationship	After you separated/ divorced	Minimizing, Denying, Blaming
1 2 3 4 5 6 7	1 2 3 4 5 6 7	1. Your ex "monopolized your perception"[2]; that is, he tried to take over your senses, making you feel crazy by trying to distort what you knew, remembered, saw, thought, or felt. For example, he minimized the extent to which he hurt you, denied hurting you, or blamed you for making him hurt you.
1 2 3 4 5 6 7	1 2 3 4 5 6 7	2. Your ex said the abuse didn't happen or "forgot" about it. For example, he said, "I don't know what you're talking about" or "you're crazy."[1]
1 2 3 4 5 6 7	1 2 3 4 5 6 7	3. Your ex made light of the abuse.[1] For example, said "it wasn't that bad," "everyone fights like this," "You're always so dramatic," "you're getting upset about nothing," or "*I'm* not upset."
1 2 3 4 5 6 7	1 2 3 4 5 6 7	4. Your ex blamed you for his problems. For example, he said that if you "believed in him" he would be more successful.[8]

1 2 3 4 5 6 7	1 2 3 4 5 6 7	5. You felt guilty when your ex blamed you for the abuse, believing that it's *your* job to keep the family happy.[8]
1 2 3 4 5 6 7	1 2 3 4 5 6 7	6. Your ex blamed an outside event or situation for the abuse. For example, he blamed his actions on being drunk or using drugs, a problem at work, a disagreement, or financial worries.[8]
1 2 3 4 5 6 7	1 2 3 4 5 6 7	7. Your ex blamed you for the abuse. For example, he said "I've had enough of your nagging" or "You're always trying to pick a fight" or "It takes two to fight," or he says if you'd done what he asked, you wouldn't have gotten hurt.[5]
1 2 3 4 5 6 7	1 2 3 4 5 6 7	8. Your ex spoke against you to everyone in town.[6]
1 2 3 4 5 6 7	1 2 3 4 5 6 7	9. You began to accept your ex's version of reality, and began to believe that the abuse was your fault, that it wasn't "that bad," or that the relationship wasn't really abusive, after all.[8]
1 2 3 4 5 6 7	1 2 3 4 5 6 7	10. Your ex blames your family or the children for the abuse.[5]
1 2 3 4 5 6 7	1 2 3 4 5 6 7	11. Your ex wouldn't take your concerns about the abuse seriously. For example, he refused to talk about problems, or responded with, "You're making a mountain out of a molehill."[8]
1 2 3 4 5 6 7	1 2 3 4 5 6 7	12. Your ex tells you what you need to do to keep him from having to abuse you again.[5]
1 2 3 4 5 6 7	1 2 3 4 5 6 7	13. You felt grateful for your ex's explanation of reality; because it helped you make sense of what was going on.[8]

1 2 3 4 5 6 7	1 2 3 4 5 6 7	14. Your ex treats periodic improvements in his behavior or stretches of non-abusive times as a reason or excuse for abuse. For example, he may say, "I haven't done anything like that in a long time, so why are you making a big deal out of it." [15]

How does he do that?

When I meet this type of coercive controller, I easily catch on to what he is doing because he never wants to take responsibility for his own actions. He presents as a wonderful, charming, supportive man who will sweep you off your feet and take you hostage before you even have time to get to know him. He falls in love with you at first sight and tells you everything he thinks you want to hear.

He uses his charm to hook you into paying attention only to him until he gains control over you. Then, he switches and starts to minimize and blame you for anything that goes wrong. He denies he has any responsibility for whatever goes wrong in your relationship. You are always the cause for his abuse toward you. Even his apologies involve blaming you for his actions.

By the time you are his hostage, it is often too late to walk away easily. You may be married so fast, you feel like he "swept you off your feet." On the other hand, you may find yourself pregnant and do not have any way to care for yourself and your baby. Another way he takes you hostage is to guilt you into staying with him. He may say he gave up a special job just to be with you, or no one in his family ever was divorced so how could you do this to his family, or he "loves you so much" he could never love anyone else. If you leave him, he will be alone forever. All these reasons provide him the ammunition to minimize, deny, and blame you for his coercive control over you.

He may see you as weak or needy and view himself as your "knight in shining armor that has come to rescue you." He may promise to support you so you can give up your job and just stay home and take care of him. He may show insane jealousy when you first tell him you are pregnant or, just the opposite, he may engage in reproductive abuse to coerce you into becoming pregnant. Then he will expect you to be eternally grateful to him and demand you can never leave him and take *his* children away from him.

When you finally get the courage to leave him, you may look back and realize you never knew him. Your whirlwind romance was based totally on the attention he gave you. He was never interested in sharing his true self with you or letting you know what makes him tick. He was only interested in you to find out your vulnerabilities so he could use them against you. You think you loved him because he was so caring and supportive in the beginning, but what you really loved was all the attention he focused on you. Do you really know enough about him to consider him a friend? Was he ever really there for you or was he just there for himself? When you use your Transformational Journaling™ Focus Points™, these are good questions to ask yourself.

Another area where I find a "Wolf in Sheep's Clothing" is around abuse of the children. This often comes out during custody battles, when the child feels safe enough to disclose physical or sexual abuse. The child discloses the abuse to you. Then you, the protective mother, report to Child Protection Services or the Family Court judge the information your child told you. The coercive controller may successfully deny his behavior by deflecting the attention from himself and onto you.

Immediately, your ex goes on the defensive and accuses you of making "false allegations" because he would "never do that to his child." He is so charming and convincing while you are so emotionally upset because you never saw what was happening (because he was real good at putting fear into your child about what would happen if your child ever told anyone) that you come across looking mentally deranged. The judge and court-appointed professionals may turn all this against you; recommend he get custody of the children, and then require you to do supervised visits. This exact situation has happened to many protective mothers who were simply trying to protect their children.

Take a few minutes now to reflect on Minimization, Denial, and Blaming coercive control patterns you identified. Compare what happened during your relationship with what is happening currently as you co-parent with your ex.

Focus Point^{TM}: What "Minimization, Denial, and Blaming" tactic patterns do you see that are similar between what happened while you were in the relationship and what is happening since you left the relationship?

Focus Point: Take each tactic you identified in the previous Focus Point^{TM} and describe in as much detail as possible how your abusive ex "Uses Minimization, Denial, or Blaming" to coercively control you.

Oftentimes, we see new patterns of Minimization, Denial, and Blaming occur after separation. This is easy for the abuser to do as he turns everything around that you bring up in court, with your attorney, or court-appointed professionals and claims it is your problem. This is the way he puts the focus on you and keeps all these highly educated people from looking at the type of person he is. When he is unable to do this, he finds other means to retaliate against you.

Identify what new Minimization, Denial, and Blaming coercive control tactics your ex is currently using.

Focus Point: What new "Minimization, Denial, or Blaming" coercive control patterns do you see your ex using since he does not have direct physical access to you?

In addition to using Minimization, Denial, and Blaming tactics with you in the courts and with court-related professionals, your ex uses these tactics in his role as a co-parent. For example, he may say that you are no longer a fit parent because you do not have a job or stable income, even though you both agreed that you would stay home and raise the children. He may accuse you of providing a lower standard of living for your children than they were accustomed to while living with both of you and argue that therefore your children should live with him. What he is not doing is being accountable to pay a reasonable settlement of property and pay adequate child support for an even distribution of the assets from your marriage. Use this opportunity to journal on how he does this.

Focus Point™: How is your ex "Using Minimization, Denial, and Blaming" coercive control patterns as a co-parent?

Examples of other protective parent's approaches to an abusive parent with the specific coercive control tactic pattern—"Using Minimization, Denial, and Blaming"

Protective mothers are often blind-sided by their ex when he implies he is going to do something, but does not discuss his intentions directly. When he actually follows through with his decision, the mother is then told that he said he was going to do ___ . Did she not understand the message he sent by e-mail, text, or left on her voice mail? He twists the situation around to make it look like she agreed to his decision when he totally ignored her response to him.

This often happens around his parenting time with the children. He will tell the mother his plans with the expectation that she will automatically agree. He does not use joint legal custody/parenting time guidelines to discuss what happens with their children. Instead, he informs the mother of his plans and expects automatic agreement. He will do this even if it is not in the "best interests of the children."

Several protective mothers shared how the father compromised their children's health. In these situations, instead of considering the mother's concerns about a child's health, the coercive controlling father chose to go through with his decision over the mother's objections. Children who experience carsickness were taken on long car trips. Children with allergies were exposed to allergens by their father, who covered up the cause rather than going to the expense of removing it. Mothers were told to stop breastfeeding so that infants could be bottle fed by their fathers during his parenting time.

These are just some examples of situations that are minimized or denied by fathers as being harmful to their children. When confronted by the protective mother, these fathers responded with verbal and emotional abuse. A coercive controlling father may do this by attacking the protective mother in e-mails, text messages, or calling her on the phone and yelling at her. He may blame her for being over-protective of their children and tell her the children would be better off with him.

Protective mothers found the process of Transformational Journaling™ helpful in venting their emotional responses to minimization, denial, and blaming. Then, they found a safe person to share their venting. This allowed them to see the best response to the coercive controlling ex by making a fact-based statement about what they know is in the "best interest of the children."

Protective mothers responded with how they cared for their children around health issues. They documented what their children's responses were to the father's choice. They kept track of any written documents to provide the courts if the situation eventually led to court involvement.

You have probably experienced many types of minimization, denial, and blaming coercive control tactics from your ex. Now, you have an opportunity to do some Transformational Journaling™ around the specific issues you identified in the assessment in this section. Use the Focus Points™ provided to help you start your journaling process. Remember, you may have additional Focus Points™ you identify to address as you journal.

These Focus points are for journaling by you on how to approach the abusive co-parent in the future related to the specific coercive control tactic—Using Minimization, Denial, and Blaming.

Focus Point™: Identify where in your life your ex is able to trigger you to respond to his demands just as he did in your relationship.

This coercive control tactic is used often by abusers after the relationship ends. Take some time to get clear on how you want to set your boundaries around Minimization, Denial, and Blaming.

Focus Point™: Determine how you want to set up healthy boundaries to protect yourself in the future from being abused through "Using Minimization, Denial, and Blaming."

Reality Check #12-- The Pompous Hog Co-Parent (Using Economic/Financial Abuse)

Using Economic/Financial Coercive Control Tactics

Economic/Financial coercive control is purposefully creating financial dependence for you on the abuser. This type of coercive control is motivated by gaining financial control over you and your children. This control and dependency is designed to prevent you from gaining economic and financial independence to care for yourself and your children. This is demonstrated by the abuser's interference in your ability to acquire and keep gainful employment, your ability to acquire and use advanced education; your ability to manage finances, and your ability to provide financial resources to support your children.

Case examples of the coercive control tactic pattern— Economic/Financial Abuse

Economic/Financial coercive control takes many forms. Here are some types of economic/financial coercive control tactics you may have in common with other protective mothers. Protective mothers may find themselves completely impoverished by the time the judge issues final orders in their court case. Protective mothers have sold their homes, sold their belongings, and put all their credit at risk just going through lengthy court battles. They may find themselves court-ordered to pay child support, legal fees, and court costs for their attempts to protect their children from a coercive controlling ex.

In some cases, mothers are jailed or warrants put out for their arrest if they are unable to make child support payments. This may effectively prevent them from being able to see their children because their ex will call law enforcement if they attempt to exercise their parenting time. Children do not understand that their mothers want to see them and be a part of their lives. They think their mothers abandoned them when the truth is that their fathers will do anything they can to interfere with their relationship with their mother.

Protective mothers who are court-ordered to have supervised visits and pay for the visits may be unable to make this happen financially. This type of economic/financial coercive control is a means the abuser uses to keep the children from having a relationship with their mother. Basically, he is retaliating against the mother for leaving him and using the children as pawns to manipulate her.

A twist on this type of economic/financial coercive control is through impoverishment of the mother so that she is unable to afford the payment for the supervisor. Another version of this type of economic/financial coercive control is for the father to agree to bring the children to a supervised visit, only to call and cancel at the last minute or not to bring the children at all. In both these instances, the mother is still required to pay the supervisor since they have scheduled the time for the visit.

Protective mothers who have given up their jobs, given up seeking a college or technical education, and agreed to stay at home and raise their children are placed at a disadvantage by the court process for determining custody/parenting time. Some of these mothers were very involved in their children's lives. They made sure they were involved in after-school activities. These mothers supported their children to develop their talents and abilities instead of seeking employment.

When these former stay-at-home moms arrive at court, they are judged harshly for not being able to financially support themselves. Many such protective mothers in this situation have lost custody/primary parenting time with their children because they were lacking financial resources. They are penalized for putting their children first and receive minimal maintenance or alimony and child support. Judges expect them to earn at least minimum wage and determine their income based on that number, even if they lack job skills.

I found protective mothers initially need empowerment and emotional support to re-establish their lives as single parents. This takes time and money. Without financial resources, these mothers fall prey to the coercive control tactics of their abusive ex. In some instances, protective mothers stay with the abuser until they are able to make life-altering shifts. In other situations, protective mothers leave their coercive controlling ex before they have the freedom to explore job possibilities or advanced education.

Your separation and pending divorce may leave you constantly fighting to catch up financially and recover emotionally. You may or may not have family to help you. Your family may be insensitive to what you have experienced and blame you for the failure of the marriage or relationship. Resources within the community are often limited if you do not have your children at least 50% of the time. As a protective mother, you may not know where to turn for help or who may be available to help you. This is where the growing number of support systems by other protective mothers is providing help.

The internet has opened the door for many protective mothers to find others in the same situation. Women empowered through the help of family and friends are able to share what helped them. This is passed on to those who are just starting to experience the economic/financial backlash of leaving a coercive controlling relationship. You may find these resources helpful in your situation. Go to Appendix A for a list of these resources.

Now, it is time for you to begin your assessment of your relationship for economic abuse while you were together and after your separation. If you prefer to print out the assessments so you can circle your responses, go to HouseOfPeacePubs.com and click on the Interpersonal Violence Assessments link to respond to the assessments. You will use what you discover with your Focus Points™.

Using Economic Abuse

1 __never, 2 __hardly ever, 3 __sometimes, 4 __often, 5 __quite often, 6 __not applicable, 7 __prefer not to answer

In the relationship	After you separated/ divorced	Economic Abuse
1 2 3 4 5 6 7	1 2 3 4 5 6 7	1. Your ex told you he would make sure you lost any job you found.[5, 10]
1 2 3 4 5 6 7	1 2 3 4 5 6 7	2. If you had a job outside the home, your ex did things to make it difficult for you to get to work. For example, he prevented you from going to work, or beat you up so badly you could not go to work or were too ashamed to show up.[5, 10]
1 2 3 4 5 6 7	1 2 3 4 5 6 7	3. Your ex did things to keep you from having money of your own. For example, he refused to buy you clothes to look for work or go to work.[5, 10]

1 2 3 4 5 6 7	1 2 3 4 5 6 7	
1 2 3 4 5 6 7	1 2 3 4 5 6 7	4. Your ex prevented you from getting a job. For example, he hid the car keys or took the car so you could not go look for a job or go to a job interview; beat you up if you said you needed or wanted to go to work.[5, 10]
1 2 3 4 5 6 7	1 2 3 4 5 6 7	5. Your ex made you ask him for money, or gave you an allowance. [5, 10]
1 2 3 4 5 6 7	1 2 3 4 5 6 7	6. Your ex demanded to know how you spent shared money.[5, 10]
1 2 3 4 5 6 7	1 2 3 4 5 6 7	7. Your ex forced you to do illegal work. For example, forced you into prostitution; forced you to sell or transport drugs; pressured you into working with him on his illegal business activities.[5, 10]
1 2 3 4 5 6 7	1 2 3 4 5 6 7	8. Your ex stole your property. For example, after moving out and getting a lawyer, he stole your car[6] and other household furnishings.[5, 10]
1 2 3 4 5 6 7	1 2 3 4 5 6 7	9. If you had a job, your ex made it difficult for you to keep it. For example, he threatened you to make you leave work; interfered in your job so you would be fired; demanded that you quit your job; threatened to contact your workplace to get you fired.[5, 10]
1 2 3 4 5 6 7	1 2 3 4 5 6 7	10. Your ex took your money.[2] For example, he took money from your purse, wallet, or bank account without your permission and/or knowledge; or took your paycheck, financial aid check, tax refund check, disability payment, or other support payments from you.[5, 10]
1 2 3 4 5 6 7	1 2 3 4 5 6 7	11. Your ex forced you to give him money or let him use your checkbook, ATM card, or credit card.[5, 10]

1 2 3 4 5 6 7	1 2 3 4 5 6 7	13. Your ex decided how you could spend money rather than letting you spend it how you saw fit.[5, 10]
1 2 3 4 5 6 7	1 2 3 4 5 6 7	14. Your ex demanded that you give him receipts and/or change when you spent money.[5, 10]
1 2 3 4 5 6 7	1 2 3 4 5 6 7	15. Your ex kept you from having the money you needed to buy food, clothes, or other necessities.[5, 10]
1 2 3 4 5 6 7	1 2 3 4 5 6 7	16. Your ex hid money so that you could not find it.[5]
1 2 3 4 5 6 7	1 2 3 4 5 6 7	17. Your ex gambled with your money or your shared money. [5, 10]
1 2 3 4 5 6 7	1 2 3 4 5 6 7	18. Your ex had you obtain money from sources other than work. For example, he made you ask your family or friends for money; made you ask for "loans" but would not let you pay them back.[5, 10]
1 2 3 4 5 6 7	1 2 3 4 5 6 7	19. Your ex convinced you to lend him money, but he would not pay it back.[5, 10]
1 2 3 4 5 6 7	1 2 3 4 5 6 7	20. Your ex kept you from having access to your bank accounts.[5, 10]
1 2 3 4 5 6 7	1 2 3 4 5 6 7	21. Your ex kept financial information from you.[5, 10]
1 2 3 4 5 6 7	1 2 3 4 5 6 7	22. Your ex made important financial decisions without talking with you about it first.[5, 10]
1 2 3 4 5 6 7	1 2 3 4 5 6 7	23. Your ex threatened you or beat you up for paying the bills or buying things that were needed.[5, 10]
1 2 3 4 5 6 7	1 2 3 4 5 6 7	24. Your ex spent the money you needed for rent or other bills.[5, 10]
1 2 3 4 5 6 7	1 2 3 4 5 6 7	25. Your ex paid bills late or did not pay bills that were in your name or in both of your names. [5, 10]
1 2 3 4 5 6 7	1 2 3 4 5 6 7	26. Your ex built up debt under your name by doing things like using your credit card or running up the phone bill.[5, 10]

1 2 3 4 5 6 7	1 2 3 4 5 6 7	27. Your ex refused to get a job so you had to support your family alone.[5, 10]
1 2 3 4 5 6 7	1 2 3 4 5 6 7	28. Your ex pawned your property or your shared property.[5, 10]
1 2 3 4 5 6 7	1 2 3 4 5 6 7	29. Your ex took your money.[2] For example, he convinced you and your boss to let him pick up your paycheck each week to put it in the bank. Then, he would not let you decide how to spend it while he was unemployed.[5]
1 2 3 4 5 6 7	1 2 3 4 5 6 7	30. Your ex deprived you of necessities such as food or medicine.[2]
1 2 3 4 5 6 7	1 2 3 4 5 6 7	31. Your ex refused to pay child support or quit his job so he was unable to pay child support or worked for cash so he did not have reportable income to pay child support[5] or sent $20 a week in child support for seven years and considered that a lordly sum.[6]
1 2 3 4 5 6 7	1 2 3 4 5 6 7	32. Your ex put you and your children in poverty through extended litigation.[6]
1 2 3 4 5 6 7	1 2 3 4 5 6 7	33. Your ex claimed your children on taxes for his economic advantage.[6]
1 2 3 4 5 6 7	1 2 3 4 5 6 7	34. After you moved out, your ex refused to sell your house and divide up the proceeds.[6]
1 2 3 4 5 6 7	1 2 3 4 5 6 7	35. When you moved out, your ex refused to let you take anything you had not paid for.[6]
1 2 3 4 5 6 7	1 2 3 4 5 6 7	36. When you started earning money, your ex demanded you pay for work-related needs. Then, with increased earnings, he demanded more of your earnings even though he paid for everything prior to your career success.[6]

How does he do that?

More than one mother told me how their ex continued court actions against them until they were completely out of money. In one case, a mother sold her home, all her major appliances, and furnishings when she remarried. Her second ex, the father of her youngest child, made sure she left their home without any furnishings or the money to replace them.

In the divorce, he used a pre-nuptial agreement to keep her from having any income from marital investments. He claimed his income was much lower than it actually was so that his maintenance and child support were lower. This mother had to start over completely without any financial compensation for what she gave up when she married him.

This form of economic/financial abuse is used very often to place fathers in a position of having more advantages that are material for the children than the mother. The courts see this as a positive, give the father primary or sole custody, and put mothers on limited parenting time. Mothers are penalized for not having the same financial abilities as the father. When it comes to quality of life for the children, this does not necessarily mean a better quality of life. In fact, children have expressed a desire to be with a loving parent over being with a financially strong parent.

Now that you have assessed the economic/financial coercive control you experienced, it is time to take a close look at the patterns and tactics used. Use your Transformational Journaling™ tools to do this. Some Focus Points™ are provided to help you with this.

Focus Point: What "Economic/Financial" tactics do you see that are similar between what happened while you were in the relationship and what is happening since you left the relationship?

Economic/financial coercive control is an issue that comes up with almost every protective parent I talk with about her situation. This is a major issue because it hinges on a stable home life for parents and children. For many protective mothers, being able to have a place to live, food for their children, and being able to provide necessities for family members is the first hurdle to cross after leaving a coercive controller. Go slowly with your Transformational Journaling™ and describe in detail how economic/financial coercive control is used against you. Allow your emotions to flow out in your journal, then be sure to share them with your confidant. Just being listened to is an important part of getting past what happened to you or may still be happening so you can make carefully thought out plans how you will become financially independent from your ex.

Focus Point: Take each tactic you identified in the previous Focus Point™ and describe in as much detail as possible how your abusive ex "Uses Economic/Financial" tactics to coercively control you. Hint: You may find it easier to complete this Focus Point™ in your journal or in a separate notebook.

You have explored in-depth the types of economic/financial control used by your ex. Take some time to identify how your ex may be continuing to use economic/financial coercive control since you separated. This is an important part of your journaling process. Make sure to go back to your confidant with what you discover.

Focus Point™: What new "Economic/ Financial" coercive control patterns do you see your ex using since he does not have direct physical access to you?

When protective mothers look at the economic/financial coercive control used by their ex around co-parenting, they tend to find a lot of emotional issues tied to this issue. It is extremely difficult for mothers to watch their children being hurt by their father's unwillingness to provide for the children following separation/divorce. Remember, coercive controlling fathers are not always interested in what is "best for their children." He may not care about helping the children maintain their standard of living after divorce. The coercive controlling father's focus is on retaliating against the mother. Therefore, if refusal to provide for the children bothers their mother, this is just another coercive control tactic based on an "I'll show you" attitude.

Focus Point: How is your ex using the economic/financial coercive control patterns as a co-parent?

Examples of other protective parent's approaches to an abusive co-parent with the specific coercive control tactic pattern—Using Economic/Financial Abuse

When the coercive controlling co-parent refuses to bring your children to supervised visits, he is retaliating against you by costing you money and time. Some protective mothers still have recourse to file motions for contempt with the court. If the court refuses to hear the petition, that is not the mother's fault. Your attempts are documented in the court record, and when your children age out of the system, they can look up the court record or come to you and find out that you did everything in your power to be able to see them.

Some abusive co-parents attempt to maintain control over their ex by going around court orders for payment of child support. These controlling co-parents may try to coerce their ex into agreements that allow him to give them money when they call him for it, may make payments in cash so the payment is not documentable, or may insist on paying a smaller amount of child support than the court ordered them to pay.

The way a protective mother can avoid these types of coercive control patterns is to ask that child support be paid through the court. This provides documentation if there is ever a need to file contempt charges for nonpayment or reduced payment of child support. If the payments are due at the beginning of the month, you may have to arrange your budget to account for the court's delay in making the money available to you. Many mothers do this by assigning the child support payment to bills for their children that come after the middle of the month. It is a simple management function you can learn to accommodate. Ultimately, you will want to get yourself in a financial situation where child support is a bonus to your income that you live on and use to support your children.

These Focus points are for journaling by you on how to approach the abusive co-parent in the future related to the specific coercive control tactic—Using Economic/Financial Abuse.

Focus Point^{TM}*: Identify where in your life your ex is able to trigger you to respond to his demands just as he did in your relationship.*

Once you identify the "Economic/ Financial" tactic patterns, then you can go on to determine what you plan to do to take care of yourself economically and financially. Some protective mothers found ways to go to school through their local community college and obtain a two-year degree. This led them onto a bachelor's degree and eventually a master's degree. Other protective mothers followed their dreams or life passions by reaching out to their local technical schools and colleges to get their certificates. Still others worked closely with counselors and advisors to help them repurpose their life experience into a strong resume that helped them move into a business environment.

No matter what your passion or dream, you can pursue it and open up the doors to accomplish your goals. Decide how you want to support yourself and go for it. You may be an entrepreneur and not even realize it. You could start your own business or provide a service in your community. You could start out doing volunteer work and end up in a well-paid position. Whatever your choice, there are multiple options. You are capable of supporting yourself and your children. Brainstorm with safe people in your support system and you will find the answers.

You may be eligible for financial resources you have not yet considered. Mothers who worked with me did not realize they were eligible to file for social security benefits based on their ex-husband's earnings. Check the social security website to see if this is an option for you. Other mothers found a variety of benefits available to them for student grants and loans. Be sure to check out the financial aid office at any college, university, or trade program you may want to attend. If you are a member of an Indian tribe or have ancestors who were, you may qualify for benefits. These are just some examples of what has worked for protective mothers.

The answers to these questions can lead you to find the right ways for you to provide for yourself. Use the following Transformational Journaling™ Focus Points™ to help you discover your dreams and passions and chart your life course.

Focus Point™: Determine how you want to set up healthy boundaries to protect yourself in the future from being abused through "Using Economic/Financial" coercive control.

Now take some time to look at your life vision moving forward from this point in time. This is a start toward defining your goals as you want them to be. Let go of all the messages about what mom, dad, or your ex expected you to be and focus on your passions, your talents and abilities.

Focus Point^{TM}: What is your plan? What are your goals? What is your life passion? Sometimes you hear this question asked as "what do you want to do, be, have, or give?"

Debra A. Wingfield, Ed.D.

Reality Check #13 -- **The Intimidating Badger Co-Parent (Using Intimidation)**

of a closet, scaring you with fake blood, plastic rodents, or snakes.

Using Intimidation Coercive Control Tactics

Intimidation is attitudes and behaviors used to summon fear of harm at the hands of the abuser. Intimation tactics are used to gain power over the victim and manipulate the victim to respond as the abuser desires even if this is counter to the victim's desires. The victim is often caught in a double-bind or Catch-22 with the abuser when she attempts to comply with his demands because he changes his demands so she can never respond correctly. Basically, no matter what you do, you can never do it right for him.

Case examples of the coercive control tactic pattern—Using Intimidation

When you are still in a relationship with an abuser who uses intimidation, you may experience some of the following coercive control tactic patterns. The abuser teaches you what he expects of you through gestures, like a shaken fist or a lifted eyebrow, to let you know you may be crossing his arbitrary line. The underlying message is that if you continue to do what you are doing, he will escalate to an increased level of control or even violence.

This type of coercive control is then used to control you in public. For instance, you may be at a party talking with female acquaintances and a male walks up to your group. Your abuser stares at you from across the room until you look at him. He clenches his fist so only you can see it. The hidden message is, you need to get away from the group or you will pay later with a beating, whether verbal or physical.

Another way he can control you is to raise his eyebrow and give you an angry look that carries the same message as above. You learn over time that if you continue talking to another male, you will pay when you get home. These types of intimidation tactics come from his extreme insecurity. He expresses this through jealousy and minimizes it or denies it by saying he "only has eyes for you" and you must do the same for him or "you must not love him."

Some men control their spouse/partner by keeping track of her throughout the day. They call, text, or e-mail whenever possible with the expectation that his partner will respond immediately to him. If you fail to respond within a few seconds, you are accused of having an affair or trying to make him jealous. This type of tracking is a different form of stalking because he covers it up by saying he just cares about you so much, he does not want to be out of touch with you for too long. In reality, he is afraid you may find him undesirable and go looking for another partner.

Since his smothering behavior may be one of the reasons you decide to leave, he feels justified in being right about predicting your behavior. He fails to see that his smothering behavior is what pushed you away from him. If you do leave and find someone else, he will create chaos in your life and your relationship to chase the new man in your life away. He believes that once you married him or partnered with him, you belong to him forever.

This type of retaliation behavior is intimidating, threatening, and controlling without him being physically present in your life. If you have children together, he takes this one step further and threatens to take you back to court if you choose to remarry. He does not want another man parenting his children and, according to him, you have no right to allow this to happen.

Other types of intimidation he uses include taking you back to court for anything he does not agree with concerning your parenting. He may threaten to get custody of the children and force you to have supervised visits because you are "alienating" the children from him. In truth, he is pushing the children away from himself by his abusive and fear-producing behaviors.

He may intimidate the children with demeaning comments about you. Some protective mothers tell me their children are not allowed to say they love their mother in front of their father. The father tells his children "all they ever do is play up to their mother so they get what they want from her." This is his way of defining the relationship they are supposed to have with their mother, and he does not approve of this type of relationship. If the children attempt to say anything different to their father, he punishes them for talking back to him because he believes he knows better.

Some mothers tell me their children do not want to see their father, but the children are afraid to tell their father this because he will get mad. They pretend to be happy with him, then return to the mother and release all their locked up feelings. If this is happening to you, remember, your children see you as the safe parent with whom they can be themselves. Allow them time to release their feelings during the transition time between their father and you. The remainder of your parenting time will flow more smoothly and your children will be happier in your presence.

Assessment of the coercive control tactic pattern—Using Intimidation

Take a few minutes now to assess how Intimidation is/was used in your relationship. Then, we will look at how you can set healthy boundaries to keep yourself safe and your children safe from these tactic patterns in the future. It is time for you to take a careful, open-minded look at how your ex "Used Intimidation" in your relationship. Then, go back and do the assessment again to look at how your ex may still be "Using Intimidation" in your Co-Parenting relationship. You will use your journal to describe in detail how your ex used the patterns with you during your relationship and continues to use those patterns as a co-parent.

If you prefer to print out the assessments so you can circle your responses, go to HouseOfPeacePubs.com and click on the Interpersonal Violence Assessments link to respond to the assessments. You will use what you discover with your Focus Points[TM].

Using Intimidation

1 __never, 2 __hardly ever, 3 __sometimes, 4 __often, 5 __quite often, 6 __not applicable, 7 __prefer not to answer

In the relationship	After you separated/ divorced	Intimidation
1 2 3 4 5 6 7	1 2 3 4 5 6 7	1. Your ex embarrassed you on social occasions to get you to do as instructed.[1]
1 2 3 4 5 6 7	1 2 3 4 5 6 7	2. Your ex tells you he is only doing what is best for you while his true desire is to control you.[1]
1 2 3 4 5 6 7	1 2 3 4 5 6 7	3. Your ex revealed your personal secrets to family members or friends.[1]

1 2 3 4 5 6 7	1 2 3 4 5 6 7	4. Your ex forced you to listen to long "lectures" from him about his rules, opinions, or dissatisfaction with you at all hours. ("It's done, when I say it's done.")[1]
1 2 3 4 5 6 7	1 2 3 4 5 6 7	5. Your ex engaged in frequent sexual inspections.[1]
1 2 3 4 5 6 7	1 2 3 4 5 6 7	6. Your ex secretly monitored your cell phone.[1]
1 2 3 4 5 6 7	1 2 3 4 5 6 7	7. Your ex openly followed you[1] or had you followed.
1 2 3 4 5 6 7	1 2 3 4 5 6 7	8. Your ex made statements that caused your children to worry on your behalf. For example, told the children in front of you, "If your mother isn't here when you come home from school, look under the ground in the backyard, right where the dog is buried."[2]
1 2 3 4 5 6 7	1 2 3 4 5 6 7	9. Your ex called you repeatedly at work or showed up there unexpectedly.[1]
1 2 3 4 5 6 7	1 2 3 4 5 6 7	10. Your ex sent anonymous "reports" about your sex life, alcohol use, child abuse, or other behavior (either true or untrue) to clients, business associates, coworkers, family members, or friends.[1]
1 2 3 4 5 6 7	1 2 3 4 5 6 7	11. Your ex described in detail how he could have killed you without being found out.[1]
1 2 3 4 5 6 7	1 2 3 4 5 6 7	12. Your ex gave you the "silent treatment" (sometimes for long periods of time) after you refused a demand or otherwise displeased him.[1]

1 2 3 4 5 6 7	1 2 3 4 5 6 7	13. Your ex cleaned house by burning toys, pieces of furniture, or your clothing.[1]
1 2 3 4 5 6 7	1 2 3 4 5 6 7	14. Your ex's rage was red hot, volcanic.[6]
1 2 3 4 5 6 7	1 2 3 4 5 6 7	15. Your ex read your text messages, e-mail, Facebook page comments, journals, diaries, or blogs (Cyberstalking).[1]
1 2 3 4 5 6 7	1 2 3 4 5 6 7	16. Your ex drove recklessly with you and/or the children in the car.[1]
1 2 3 4 5 6 7	1 2 3 4 5 6 7	17. Your ex allowed children to have "accidents" while he was caring for (or "babysitting") them.[1]
1 2 3 4 5 6 7	1 2 3 4 5 6 7	18. Your ex checked your phone calls, and called back anyone whose voice he did not recognize.[1]
1 2 3 4 5 6 7	1 2 3 4 5 6 7	19. Your ex made you feel crazy by sabotaging a common activity (e.g., turning off the stove after you turned it on; moving your car without your knowledge; or putting your car keys in a strange place).[1]
1 2 3 4 5 6 7	1 2 3 4 5 6 7	20. Your ex told you when he was hurting you, "You're the person I want to hurt."[6]
1 2 3 4 5 6 7	1 2 3 4 5 6 7	21. Your ex ransacked where you worked, fire-bombed or damaged your new partner's home in some way, made threats to you and your new partner.[6]

1 2 3 4 5 6 7	1 2 3 4 5 6 7	22. Your ex played cruel jokes on you or frightened you and excused his behavior by calling it "fun" or "games." For example, he surprised you by practical jokes such as jumping out of a closet, scaring you with fake blood, plastic rodents, or snakes. and excused it as "a joke"; he plays too roughly with young children and excuses it as "games."[1]
1 2 3 4 5 6 7	1 2 3 4 5 6 7	23. Your ex performed, in secret, any action that you knew you couldn't bring attention to because you would then be more at risk for further emotional or physical abuse.[1] For example, he intentionally damaged your car, but you didn't mention it for fear he would wreck it; you're sure he followed you to work, but you didn't complain, for fear that next time he would talk to your boss and you might lose your job.
1 2 3 4 5 6 7	1 2 3 4 5 6 7	24. You understand and accept your ex's reasons for wanting to make you fearful of injury or harm. You feel grateful when your partner warns you when you are "out of line." Or, you feel grateful when your partner gives you a brief break from feeling frightened.[6]

1 2 3 4 5 6 7	1 2 3 4 5 6 7	25. Your ex refused to divorce you and then agreed to pay your rent and minimal child support if you never have another affair.[6]
1 2 3 4 5 6 7	1 2 3 4 5 6 7	26. After you were divorced, your ex found out you went on a date, threatened your date, or called your date's parents, or stopped sending rent money until you were evicted while he remarried and had another family, or similar circumstances.[6]

How does he do that?

One protective mother shared with me that her ex or someone that he had encouraged reported her to social services for having an unclean home. Even though he had not been in the home nor had the other person who made the report, Child Protection Services did come to her home. They required the mother to do some cleanup in her home that she was already in the process of doing. This put undue pressure on her to fulfill their demands and added to the stress that she was under in her attempts to protect her children.

In addition to making this unwarranted call to Child Protection Services, the mother encountered a "potential reporter" on the street and was intimidated further by the reporter when she asked the mother, "How did you like your visit from child protection?" The intimidation did not stop there. It was also carried over onto Facebook, where negative comments about the mother were posted and read by other members of the community. Initially, the mother felt some people in the community backing off from making connections with her. However, this seemed to die down quickly as she continued to maintain her confidence and composure in the community.

An abuser's use of other individuals to be involved in his intimidating behaviors is designed to keep the mother constantly on guard for further attacks. This type of stress is often translated to the children because the mother is distracted. One way to overcome this type of distraction is to shut down as many connections as possible with friends, family, and acquaintances of the abuser. There is no point in monitoring the abuser's behavior although the protective mother may feel this is one way to know whether she is safe.

Alternatively, protective mothers can learn tools and skills to protect themselves and their children without keeping tabs on their ex. The Transformational Journaling™ tools provided in this book can help you identify other healthy ways to protect yourself and your children. Before you address the types of intimidation tactics used by your ex in his co-parenting, it is helpful to go back and review your responses to the assessment in this section.

Here are some Focus Points™ to help you sort out the intimidation tactic patterns used by your ex.

Focus Point™: What Intimidation patterns do you see that are similar between what happened while you were in the relationship and what is happening since you left the relationship?

Describe in detail how your ex is using these patterns directly with you or indirectly through your children. One mother related that her ex gave the child support check to one of their children instead of sending it to her or making the payment through the court. The message was that he would control when, where, and to whom he was going to pay child support. She was very happy to hear my recommendation that she ask her attorney to arrange child support payments made through the court.

Focus Point™: How is your ex using Intimidation patterns as a co-parent?

This Focus Point™ is for your journaling on how to approach the abusive parent in the future related to the specific coercive control tactic—Using Intimidation.

Focus Point™: Identify where in your life your ex is able to trigger you to respond to his demands just as he did in your relationship.

Examples of how other protective parents approach an abusive parent with the specific coercive control tactic pattern—Using Intimidation

Once you identify the intimidation tactic patterns your ex is using in his co-parenting with you, you have taken the first step to stop his behavior from affecting you. He may continue to use intimidation tactics while you refuse to respond to those tactics.

For example, if he uses threatening gestures when he sees you in the community, you can choose to ignore those gestures as if they never occurred. Because he is not getting a reaction from you with those gestures, over time, he may cease using those gestures. If your children see him using those gestures, and they express fear or concern because of his behavior, you can help your children learn that some people do not have good communication skills to express their feelings and they use angry gestures instead. Let your children know that you are not afraid of your ex and the gestures he is making and that you are working to make sure the children are safe and protected from his anger.

If your ex has threatened your children and they report the abuse to you, let your children know that you will do everything possible to keep them safe from him and from further abuse. Because the reality is that courts and court-appointed personnel often make a mistake when they fail to believe these children, you need to repeatedly tell your children that you are doing everything possible to keep them safe. If the courts require the children to have parenting time with their abuser, do everything you possibly can to make sure this happens in a supervised setting. Be sure to document all your children's concerns and behaviors when they are required to see their father. Ask supervisors to document your children's statements and behaviors as well.

Establish clear boundaries to set for yourself when your ex Uses Intimidation Tactics

Focus Point^{TM}: Determine how you want to set up healthy boundaries to protect yourself in the future from being abused through "Using Intimidation".

Reality Check #14-- **The Threatening Skunk Co-Parent (Using Threats and Coercion)**

Using Threats and Coercion Coercive Control Tactics

Threats and Coercion are attitudes and behaviors used to force the victim into doing what the abuser demands under threat of loss of something or someone special to the victim or threat of bodily injury. These attitudes and behaviors are used to gain power over the victim and force the victim to respond to the abuser's desires without question. The problem is the consequences may be life-threatening or lead to death. If you are still in a relationship with an abuser who uses coercion and threats, you may find some of the coercive control tactic patterns you experience are discussed here.

Case examples of the coercive control tactic pattern—Using Threats and Coercion

Many protective mothers have stayed in abusive relationships much longer than is safe for them and their children. Although judges and other professionals sometimes fail to understand this type of behavior, protective mothers tell me that their abusers' threats to take the children away forever, or threats to kill her, the children, and himself are issued with such adamant certainty that it is hard for her to believe he will do anything else. For protective mothers, these threats are very real and so believable that it is difficult for a protective mother to see that she has a safe way out.

One protective mother shared with me her concerns about her daughters and their safety if she was not present in the home to protect them. She felt it was better to remain in the relationship to keep her children safe rather than leaving the home and taking the chance that they would be hurt while alone with their father. When this protective mother did decide to leave her marriage, she left because her older daughter revealed sexual abuse being perpetrated on her by her father.

Professionals documented the abuse, then, the children were only required to see their father in a supervised setting. The children were so traumatized by the father's abuse of them that even in a supervised setting they refused to see him. The mother made every attempt possible to encourage her daughters to see their father in that setting and was unsuccessful.

At the end of the required time for supervised visits with the father, the children were still refusing to have any contact with him. Their night terrors and nightmares continued, and his threatening gestures when seeing their mother around town continued to reinforce their fear of him. The intensity of the threats the father made to his daughters when he was abusing them carried over to their responses to other men in the community.

This type of trauma requires protective mothers to continually demonstrate to the court the impact on their children. The protective mother described above has many years to go before her children age out of the system and are no longer under the reign of terror from their father while he continues to pursue custody of them. Other types of threats received by protective mothers may include threats issued through emails, text messages, voicemails, and threatening telephone calls.

Another mother I support continually receives threatening emails from her ex whenever she does not immediately agree with his demands "according to the court order." This particular father attempts to coerce his ex into complying with his demands by threatening to take her back in front of the judge if she does not readily agree with him. This coercive behavior is designed to force her back in line with his way of thinking and attempts to control her involvement with their child. What is actually happening here is the father is demanding his parental "rights" take priority over the best interests of his child.

This type of threatening and coercive behavior is very common among co-parenting fathers who use coercive control tactics to manipulate their ex. The father puts his self-interests above those of the child, and the child's needs are secondary to his needs. His main concern is maintaining control of his ex and the children.

The difficulties that arise from this type of coercive control tactic for the protective mother is her constantly having to weigh the best interests of her children over the potential negative manipulations of the father. If the father makes good on his threats to take her back to court, she may lose more of her parenting time, he may gain sole custody/parenting time with the children, and the protective mother may be given supervised visits. The problem here, as in many cases, is the father abuses the mother's visits and stops bringing the children or interferes in her relationship with the children.

Assessment of the coercive control tactic pattern—Using Threats and Coercion

It is time for you to take a careful, open-minded look at how your ex "Used Threats and Coercion" in your relationship. Then, go back and do the assessment again to look at how your ex may still be "Using Threats and Coercion" in your co-parenting relationship.

You will use your journal to describe in detail how your ex used the patterns with you during your relationship and continues to use those patterns as a co-parent.

If you prefer to print out the assessments so you can circle your responses, go to HouseOfPeacePubs.com and click on the Interpersonal Violence Assessments link to respond to the assessments. You will use what you discover with your Focus Points™.

Using Threats and Coercion

1 __never, 2 __hardly ever, 3 __sometimes, 4 __often, 5 __quite often, 6 __not applicable, 7 __prefer not to answer

In the relationship	After you separated/ divorced	Threats & Coercion
1 2 3 4 5 6 7	1 2 3 4 5 6 7	1. Your ex threatened to have the children taken away.[1]
1 2 3 4 5 6 7	1 2 3 4 5 6 7	2. Your ex threatened to hurt the children.[1]
1 2 3 4 5 6 7	1 2 3 4 5 6 7	3. Your ex threatened to have you committed,[1] arrested, or deported.
1 2 3 4 5 6 7	1 2 3 4 5 6 7	4. Your ex threatened friends or family.[1]
1 2 3 4 5 6 7	1 2 3 4 5 6 7	5. Your ex threatened to destroy things you cared about.[1]
1 2 3 4 5 6 7	1 2 3 4 5 6 7	6. Your ex threatened to harm or kill you, and at all times carried or had readily available the means to do so. For example, he carried a knife or kept a loaded gun within reach.[1]
1 2 3 4 5 6 7	1 2 3 4 5 6 7	7. Your ex made sure that you didn't smoke or drink during pregnancy.[5]
1 2 3 4 5 6 7	1 2 3 4 5 6 7	8. Your ex forced you to use street drugs, alcohol, or non-prescribed prescription drugs.[4]

1 2 3 4 5 6 7	1 2 3 4 5 6 7	9. Your ex used verbal abuse that brought you to tears, then made fun of your emotional pain or your tear-stained appearance.[5]
1 2 3 4 5 6 7	1 2 3 4 5 6 7	10. Your ex made fun of what you do for enjoyment.[5]
1 2 3 4 5 6 7	1 2 3 4 5 6 7	11. Your ex told people you were an unfit mother.[6]
1 2 3 4 5 6 7	1 2 3 4 5 6 7	12. Your ex threatened or hurt anyone who implicitly criticized him by defending *your* behavior.[2] For example, he beat up a friend for saying, "Your wife treats you like a prince;" told your concerned friends to "stay out of our business if they know what's good for them."
1 2 3 4 5 6 7	1 2 3 4 5 6 7	13. Your ex made vague statements that implied he was upset. You know your partner so well that he didn't have to finish making the threat for you to know that you were at risk.[5] For example, he said, "You made me jealous" and he didn't have to finish the threat by saying "and when we're home, alone, I'll make you sorry for it," because you already know.
1 2 3 4 5 6 7	1 2 3 4 5 6 7	14. Your ex damaged property, implying that you also could be damaged. For example, he helped you "redecorate" by taking a sledge-hammer to the wall; damaged a dashboard; put a fist through a windshield or wall.[1]
1 2 3 4 5 6 7	1 2 3 4 5 6 7	15. Your ex referred to what he knew about how to hurt people as an indirect way to threaten you.[5] For example, "I just watched a television program *where they showed how not to leave marks*."

1 2 3 4 5 6 7	1 2 3 4 5 6 7	16. Your ex screamed and cursed at you either in person or on the phone as a way to convince you to do what he wishes.[5]
1 2 3 4 5 6 7	1 2 3 4 5 6 7	17. Your ex required you to live in specific locations or move for his convenience.[4]
1 2 3 4 5 6 7	1 2 3 4 5 6 7	18. Your ex committed violence against strangers, friends, or property.[5]
1 2 3 4 5 6 7	1 2 3 4 5 6 7	19. Your ex used to communicate what he is capable of doing if you fall out of favor, or try to get help.[5]
1 2 3 4 5 6 7	1 2 3 4 5 6 7	20. Your ex made threats that were understood by you and that other people might not notice or see as threats.[5] For example, he gave signs of disapproval by raising an eyebrow, a clenched fist seen only by you, or tapping his fingers.
1 2 3 4 5 6 7	1 2 3 4 5 6 7	21. You understood and accepted your ex's reasons for threatening you, or trying to get you to do things his way. You felt grateful and/or loved when your partner was so intently focused on you. Or, you felt thankful to your partner for leaving you alone at times.[5]
1 2 3 4 5 6 7	1 2 3 4 5 6 7	22. Your ex showed control in ways other people may see as kind. For example, says he will make sure you eat a healthy diet during pregnancy.[5]
1 2 3 4 5 6 7	1 2 3 4 5 6 7	23. Your ex called you a whore during the custody trial.[6]
1 2 3 4 5 6 7	1 2 3 4 5 6 7	24. Your ex threatened to have your mother declared mentally incompetent if you didn't give up your claim to the children.[6]

How does he do that?

Threats and coercion are closely tied to intimidation tactics. The abuser is making every effort to secure your compliance with his demands. Some of the ways that he does this is through direct threats that he says through his voice, email, or text messages. He may tell you he has information on you that he will tell a judge so the judge will commit you to an insane asylum, or Child Protection Services will take your children away from you, or he will gain sole custody of the children by proving to the court that you are an unfit mother.

His tone of voice and his attitude are extremely convincing when he is making these threats. It leaves you with no doubt in your mind that he can actually carry them out. He may stalk you or watch you from a distance if there is a protection order in place. His mere presence in the area where you live, work, or shop serves as a threat to what he could do to you.

He lets you know in multiple ways during the relationship that he has the physical ability to harm you. He may destroy some of your property, kick the dog, or even knock holes in the wall right next to your head. The message is that the next time instead of destroying property or hurting an animal, he will actually hurt you.

If he has physically abused you, beaten you, or hurt you physically in the past, he may tell you that the next time he will take it out on one of the children. Many mothers report that they remain in abusive relationships so long as the children are unharmed. However, when he threatens or actually physically abuses the children, this is the point when she chooses to leave.

Often, after a protective mother leaves with her children, they will report to her that "daddy's been abusing us". The child abuse, while the mother remained in the relationship with the coercive controller, may be physical and sometimes sexual. If a coercive controlling father threatened the children that he would kill or harm their mother if they told her about the abuse, the children will be afraid to say anything until after mother removes them from the situation.

Mothers are often very surprised by these revelations from their children. When they look back at the situation, they often recognize that some of the children's behaviors were signals that they were being abused. This response from mothers is not surprising; after all, their focus was on protecting the children and keeping the abuser focused on her. Protective mothers often believe they can take whatever the abuser dishes out because they are adults whereas the children would not know how to handle the abuser. Part of a mother's healing is to realize she was doing everything that she could do to protect her children and that her best choice was to leave.

If this is true for your situation, remember that we know from multiple studies that mothers actually become better parents once they leave an abusive relationship. They usually are able to care for their children and to meet their emotional, physical, and social needs. Protective mothers do their very best to keep their children from being further traumatized by their abusive father. This may become more difficult if the family courts become involved. We will discuss this aspect of coercive control tactics in later sections of this book.

Now it is time for you to use your Transformational Journaling™ Focus Points™ to identify the patterns of threats and coercion used in by your abusive ex.

Focus Point™: What patterns of threats and Coercion do you see that are similar between what happened while you were in the relationship and what is happening since you left the relationship?

This Focus Points™ is for your journaling on how to approach the abusive parent in the future related to the specific coercive control tactic—Using Threats and Coercion.

Focus Point™: Identify where in your life your ex is able to trigger you to respond to his demands just as he did in your relationship.

Examples of how other protective mothers approach an abusive father with the specific coercive control tactic pattern—Using Threats and Coercion

Mothers who receive threatening emails, text messages, or phone calls from an abusive ex find it is helpful to listen past the emotional message to find the facts. Once they have identified the facts that are the focus of the communication around their children, they only respond to the facts. This can be difficult at first because there is a desire to express their feelings as well.

When we work together, protective mothers learn how to do the two-step process. First, they learn to vent their feelings in safe ways. Second, they learn how to respond to the abuser by stating only the facts that relate to their children, omitting emotional content. This two-step method protects the mothers and the children from further threats and attacks by their abusive ex.

These Focus points are for journaling by you on how to approach the abusive co-parent in the future related to the specific coercive control tactic—Using Threats and Coercion.

Focus Point™: Determine how you want to set up healthy boundaries to protect yourself in the future from being abused through "Using Threats and Coercion".

Debra A. Wingfield, Ed.D.

Reality Check #15-- **The Laughing Hyena Co-Parent (Using Isolation)**

Overview of the coercive control tactic pattern-Using Isolation

Using Isolation is defined as attitudes and behaviors designed to restrict your movements and maintain physical and emotional control of you. The abuser focuses on detaching you from contact or communication with anyone who is supportive or involved in your life. The purpose of isolation is to monopolize your attention and keep you occupied with only the information and input you receive from him.

His focus is on keeping you away from your family, friends, or other supportive people in your life. He may prevent you from making friends or keeping friends. He may take up all of your time and energy so you are unable to spend time with anyone else.

Case examples of the coercive control tactic pattern—Using Isolation

Some of the typical examples of Using Isolation Tactics include interfering with your relationships with family members, especially parents and close siblings. One protective mother shared with me how her husband limited her contact with her parents by refusing to let them come any farther than the front porch of the house. This meant that visits with her parents either had to take place outside the home in public locations or required a trip to her parents' home.

Other protective mothers shared how their visits were limited by the amount of time that they could be at their parents' home. They were timed from when they left until they arrived back home. Very often, this would only leave 10 to 15 minutes of actual time for contact with her family, regardless of the purpose of the visit. If she wanted to take her children to visit their grandparents, those visits were extremely limited by the deadline for returning home.

Other types of isolating behaviors include refusal to provide home telephone service or cell phone service for the protective mother. The abuser may use the excuse that they cannot afford home telephone service while he maintains he must have a cell phone in order to be reached by his boss. Therefore, the mother is without any means to contact emergency personnel if something happens to her or one of the children unless the father is home.

Other ways abusers isolate their partners or wives are to leave them without any type of transportation. One Colorado woman who finally was free of her abusive relationship (because he had been arrested and a restraining order prohibited him from coming close to her) found herself isolated in a small trailer. She thought she had to remain in the trailer until the lease ran out before she could find a place to live that was on a public transportation line. A victim advocate told this woman about the Colorado law that allowed her to leave her rental property before the lease was up. If the advocate had not informed her of this particular law, she would have felt trapped in the trailer until the lease expired.

If you are unfamiliar with the laws in your state regarding domestic violence, contact your local domestic violence services program or your statewide coalition to find out whether you are being isolated because you feel trapped in your rental situation. Be sure to check the resources in Appendix A at the end of this book for hotline numbers that will help you contact your statewide coalition. They will connect you with local victim services programs.

Assessment of the coercive control tactic pattern—Using Isolation

Now it is time for you to take a look at how your ex-partner/husband used isolation in your relationship while you were in the relationship and since you left the relationship. Take into consideration how isolation was used with you as well as with your children.

If you prefer to print out the assessments so you can circle your responses, go to HouseOfPeacePubs.com and click on the Interpersonal Violence Assessments link to respond to the assessments. You will use what you discover with your Focus Points[TM].

Using Isolation

1 __never, 2 __hardly ever, 3 __sometimes, 4 __often, 5 __quite often, 6 __not applicable, 7 __prefer not to answer

In the relationship	After you separated/ divorced	Using Isolation
1 2 3 4 5 6 7	1 2 3 4 5 6 7	1. Your ex stopped you from calling family or friends.[1]
1 2 3 4 5 6 7	1 2 3 4 5 6 7	2. Your ex destroyed mementos or photographs of family members.[1]
1 2 3 4 5 6 7	1 2 3 4 5 6 7	3. You cut *yourself* off from friends and family to prevent rages[1] or to keep from having to explain your every move.
1 2 3 4 5 6 7	1 2 3 4 5 6 7	4. Your ex timed or limited your conversations.[1]

1 2 3 4 5 6 7	1 2 3 4 5 6 7	5. Your ex closed off opportunities for transportation. For example, prevented you from getting a driver's license, never left the car or keys with you, monitored your trip mileage, would not provide money for public transportation.[5]
1 2 3 4 5 6 7	1 2 3 4 5 6 7	6. You found yourself avoiding accidental social contact to keep your partner or ex from becoming angry or to prevent jealous rages.[1]
1 2 3 4 5 6 7	1 2 3 4 5 6 7	7. Your ex confined you. For example, kept you in walk-in closets or specific rooms; barred you from leaving the house; made you sit in cars for hours; forced you to sit without moving on the couch or on the floor; did not permit you to drive or to go out by yourself.[2]
1 2 3 4 5 6 7	1 2 3 4 5 6 7	8. Your ex isolated you from sources of support.[2] For example, he kept you away from friends, family, church members, health care workers, or government agencies like social services.
1 2 3 4 5 6 7	1 2 3 4 5 6 7	9. Your ex stopped you from seeing health care professionals. For example, he refused to believe you needed medical or dental care; refused to provide money for health care; refused to go with you to your appointments. Or, where he is a doctor, had an associate write prescriptions for medicines (sometimes psychiatric medicines without meeting you) so you didn't get to see another doctor.[1]
1 2 3 4 5 6 7	1 2 3 4 5 6 7	10. You understood and accepted your partner's/your ex's reasons for wanting to shield you from other people. Or, you felt grateful to your partner/ex when you were finally allowed to have contact with friends, family, or other people.[5]

1 2 3 4 5 6 7	1 2 3 4 5 6 7	11. Your ex did not physically keep you in the house, but made it impossible to leave. For example, he would not let you have house keys (you couldn't lock the house behind you, and so you didn't dare leave); would not let you use the car; or he removed the battery from the car to keep you from driving anywhere.[5]
1 2 3 4 5 6 7	1 2 3 4 5 6 7	12. Your ex kept you from socializing, seeing family members, or leaving the house.[1] For example, he stopped you from going to church or to the gym;[1] forced you to quit the home-schooling network or PTA, which was your only source of contact besides children; or forced you to quit doing other activities outside your home.[1]
1 2 3 4 5 6 7	1 2 3 4 5 6 7	13. Your ex criticized your failure to succeed, while keeping you from succeeding. For example, he complained that you don't make any money, while insisting that you do all of the housework and childcare; belittled your educational level while disrupting every effort you made to get your GED, take a class, or enroll in college.[1]
1 2 3 4 5 6 7	1 2 3 4 5 6 7	14. Your ex kept you from visiting your family or friends. For example, he would not let you drive the family vehicle; insisted that you stay with him or visit his family at holidays and refused to provide money for plane trips home[1] or for gasoline to drive to visit your family.
1 2 3 4 5 6 7	1 2 3 4 5 6 7	15. Your ex prevented you from contacting anyone by removing electronic equipment. For example, he pulled the phone out of the wall;[1] or removed cell phones or computers from the house.

1 2 3 4 5 6 7	1 2 3 4 5 6 7	16. Your ex took your shoes or clothes to keep you from leaving your home.[5]
1 2 3 4 5 6 7	1 2 3 4 5 6 7	17. Your ex prevented you from socializing when in public. For example, he forced you to sit in one place ("and don't move") when you were at a bar;[1] made you stay in the car while he shopped or visited friends.
1 2 3 4 5 6 7	1 2 3 4 5 6 7	18. Your ex belittled your friends. For example, he called your friends "whores,"[1] "bitches," or "bad influences."
1 2 3 4 5 6 7	1 2 3 4 5 6 7	19. Your ex prevented your escape and/or monitored your contact with other people through an unpredictable pattern of tactics. For example, the random use of rules, stalking, cyber stalking, beepers, cell phones, and other means.[2]
1 2 3 4 5 6 7	1 2 3 4 5 6 7	20. Your ex discouraged you from shopping on your own. For example, he went through your purchases and destroyed or returned things;[2] wouldn't provide money for groceries or other necessities unless he was with you when you shopped.
1 2 3 4 5 6 7	1 2 3 4 5 6 7	21. Your ex limited your willingness to do anything or go anywhere without permission because of the inspections you had to face afterwards. For example, questioning about where you went, what you did, or whom you saw. May include the use of "micro-regulation": going through your closets, drawers, mail, e-mail, web favorites, diaries or journals, phone bills, pocket books, or checkbook.[2]

How does he do that?

Ask yourself the following question. Were you restricted from having relationships with certain friends that you met through other friends or in the community? One woman started to develop a friendship with another woman who recently moved to the community. She was excited to have a friendship with someone who she was drawn to with similar interests. After a short time, her husband told her that she needed to stop seeing her new friend because "she isn't our kind of people". This woman told her new friend what her husband said and they decided to end their friendship rather than cause problems in her marriage. Sadly, she was cut off from an important support person who could have been there for her when she filed for divorce.

Abusers sometimes use isolation tactics to keep their partner's from developing friendships and support systems connected to their children. This is a combination of using isolation and using the children coercive control tactics.

These questions can help you determine if isolation and using children were combined tactics used in your relationship or in co-parenting situations. Were your children allowed to have relationships with other children from school, or children they met through summer activities? Were your children allowed to bring other children into your home, or were they only allowed to play with other children in public locations or during school and activities?

When children are restricted from bringing friends into their home, this isolates them from friends, and having friends is a crucial part of their social and emotional developmental process. By having friends visit their home, and by visiting their friends' homes, children learn that there are differences in how families function and work together.

Mothers and children who are isolated from connecting with other mothers and children in the community are cut off from potential support systems for themselves. When these support systems are unavailable, the mother becomes more isolated and finds it difficult for her to leave an abusive relationship.

Once a mother leaves the abusive relationship, she discovers that many responsibilities she met for her children now become part of joint decision-making with her ex. Joint decision-making provides the abuser an opportunity to continue with coercive control of the mother. Here is just one example of a situation that I have seen repeatedly with children's health concerns and their custodial father's refusal to respond appropriately. Observe the tactics of isolation and using children coercive control tactics when the father's power base feels threatened by his child going to the mother with a health problem instead of bringing it to him.

Let us backtrack to a conversation between a mother and daughter. A precocious, bright girl nearing her eighth birthday transitions from parenting time with father to parenting time with mother. On the transitional ride to the mother's home, approximately one hour in duration, the daughter launches immediately into what is on her mind. It is obvious her thoughts are bubbling up as if the dam has broken and all the thoughts and feelings she has bottled up need to come tumbling out.

She starts by sharing with mother that she feels closer to her mother than to her father because mother carried her inside her body. This is the child's way of telling mother that she has something important to say to mother that she did not feel comfortable telling father. Mother understands this connection and does not see it as loving one parent more than the other parent. Mother knows that each child loves each parent differently and this is a normal and healthy response.

Once this parental bond is reestablished and validated by mother, her daughter moves directly to the real issue. The daughter explains her concerns about her health – bumps on her skin that have not cleared up with the cream father has been putting on them for four months. Mother calmly reassures her daughter they will watch the bumps over the weekend and make a doctor's appointment on Monday if there is no improvement. Mother hides her unhappiness with the way father handled the situation.

After her daughter was in bed, this mother contacted me to express her frustration and disappointment about the father's failure to seek medical attention for their daughter. I supported her monitoring her daughter over the weekend to see if her daughter's skin cleared up and her plan to call the doctor first thing Monday if there had been no improvement. We agreed it would be appropriate to wait until Monday to notify the father of her plan.

Since there was no improvement in the daughter's skin condition over the weekend, mother arranged an appointment with the doctor that day. Mother accepted the primary care physician's recommendation and agreed to schedule an appointment with a specialist. Mother notified father by e-mail that the skin condition is still present and has not changed over the weekend. She tells him she took the child to the doctor and reported the doctor's concerns and recommendations for an appointment with a specialist. The doctor's office contacted the specialist and made an appointment at the first available time. This was arranged where the doctor went to a community halfway between mother's and father's homes.

Father asserted his isolation coercive control by calling the specialist's office and scheduling an appointment the day before the appointment that had been scheduled. He then verbally attacked the mother and accused her of lying about being able to get the appointment scheduled in the city where he lived instead of the city one hour from the mother's home. His attack appeared to come from his feeling inadequate since his daughter did not go to him, but to her mother. Father undermined mother's arrangements, even though she considered his work schedule and his needs when making a follow-up appointment with a specialist. In order to regain his court-appointed role as primary parent, he believed he needed to prove in his own mind mother was wrong.

Father's initial email back to mother was a direct attack that appeared to be motivated by his daughter's choice to tell mother about her medical concerns instead of telling father.

Mother has learned it is best to have her objective supporter review her responses to her coercive ex's emails before actually sending them out. She trusts her support person to help her present her message in a factual, non-threatening way. This keeps her safe and helps her look after the safety of her daughter. Mother is able to share her feelings with her supporter and have them validated without putting herself or her daughter at risk.

In reviewing father's emails, it is clear he escalated the situation into much more than it was. His obvious sarcasm and demeaning mother by "inviting" her to attend the appointment he made showed his disdain for her and any type of meaningful relationship with their daughter. He was only concerned about asserting his "parenting time" – a parent-centered approach. This is the opposite of the mother's expression of "parental concern" – a child-centered approach.

In the discussion with her support person, mother decided it would be best not to respond to father's last email since his pattern was to always have the last word. She expressed her concerns for her child's emotional safety on her transition back to father's parenting time. Mother and her support person discussed her concerns that their child's father might interrogate their daughter; possibly threaten her to only tell him her concerns and not mother. Mother also experienced father's physical violence during their marriage and expressed concerns about him getting physically abusive with their daughter.

Mother talked about options of how to educate her daughter about what to do if she felt threatened without creating bias against the father. Mother decided she would teach her daughter to use her cell phone to call 911 if her daughter ever felt unsafe with any adult in the future. Mother reviewed a power and control wheel about children and the nurturing parent wheel (See Appendix A for power and control wheels) as well. Mother was supported and her feelings validated by her support person in this situation. She was encouraged to handle the transition from parent to parent in the same manner she handles it each week.

This is just one example of how a father used isolation coercive control with the children to undermine the mother/child relationship. Fathers who "Use the Children" to retaliate against their former spouse/partner to Isolate the children from the mother/child relationship often find the children unwilling to have parenting time with them. This coercive isolation is then turned around on the mother and she is blamed for "alienating" the children from him.

His response is to use Litigation Abuse and Family Court Abuse (discussed in section III)to obtain full custody/parenting time with the children and mother may be required to have supervised visits so her time with the children will be significantly reduced. The harm to children from this parent-centered approach has the opposite response for fathers. They fail to realize they cannot force their children to love them or want to be with them if they are using coercive control tactics with them. Ultimately, when the children reach adolescence or adulthood, they back away from ongoing relationships with their father.

How to respond to the coercive control tactic—Using Isolation

Use the following focus point to describe new patterns your ex uses to isolate you now that you are out of the relationship. These may be ways of isolating you from your family, your children, or interfering in these relationships.

Focus Point: What new patterns do you see your ex using since he does not have direct contact with you?

Use the following Focus Point™ to describe how your ex is Using Isolation in his co-parent relationship with you.

Focus Point: How is your ex using Isolation patterns as a co-parent?

This Focus Point™ is for your journaling on how to approach the abusive parent in the future related to the specific coercive control tactic-Isolation.

Focus Point: Identify where in your life your ex is able to trigger you to respond to his demands just as he did in your relationship.

Focus Point: Determine how you want to set up healthy boundaries to protect yourself in the future from being abused through "Using Isolation."

Examples of how other protective parents approach an abusive parent with the specific coercive control tactic pattern—Using Isolation

Here is an idea of how I provided support to the mother in the doctor appointment situation.

Here is the e-mail I sent to mother as her supporter.

"M,

Venting is definitely the first step to keep yourself from saying something that will escalate him. The next step is to respond that you appreciate him giving you such advance notice and that you checked your calendar and that works for you as well.

What you are doing by this is slowly shaping his thinking about how to co-parent rather than issuing proclamations that you have no say in. This process is what we do with anyone with Cognitive Distortions. It is called Cognitive Restructuring. (These are terms the mother is learning about as she pursues her bachelor's degree.)

Remember, you are responding, not reacting, to what he is saying. He is unaccustomed to this because he only knows how to communicate ineffectively whereas you are learning to communicate effectively without being drawn into a fight. Therefore, he does not get the payoff he wants because you don't engage in his fight. This form of behavior modification leads to what we call "an extinction burst." He no longer continues to communicate this way because it doesn't get him what he wants. This is not an overnight process so stick with it and give it time to work. Meanwhile, keep venting to me :>)

Debra"

Here is how M replied to F when he denied M the ability to pick up the daughter at school for the doctor appointment.

"*F*

I am pleased that she will be getting in sooner. If you choose to pick her up that is fine, however, I plan on being there. This is a concern parental issue not a parental time issue. It is disheartening to see that you feel that I should not be included in daughter's important events, include [sic] her medical needs. I have nothing to gain by your accusations of lying, I will be traveling ether [sic] way, I merely informed you of what was told

*to me. None the less the most important thing is daughter's health.
The Doctor who saw her is her primary doctor now. Dr. __.*

M"

Please note in this case the appointment father manipulated with
the doctor's office was one day before the appointment mother was
given when the daughter's doctor arranged the appointment.
Notice how mother was supported in de-escalating father and
leaving emotions out of the communication. Mother states clearly
that this is a parental issue since they have joint legal custody that
overrides parenting time. Mother remains child-centered even
though father's statements in the prior email were clearly parent-
centered.

There were numerous e-mails back and forth on this one issue.
Mother shared her responses with me for feedback before sending
them to father. Father made various threats, including threats to go
back to court if mother pursued the matter further. His e-mails
were filled with parent-centered accusations, twisting the truth, and
failure to consider the cause of the daughter's health problems.
Mother was focused on looking at all avenues that may be the
cause of the daughter's health problems and invited F to do the
same. Mother showed a child-centered focus to the entire issue.

Notice how the father attempted to use isolation coercive control
tactics to keep mother from being involved in the health care of
their child. By arranging the appointment for mother to have to
drive two hours each way instead of one hour both ways, father
hoped to keep mother from attending the doctor's appointment. He
was attempting to isolate her from another part of her daughter's
life. Mother made the decision to attend the appointment and
future appointments their daughter had with this doctor. Mother
refused to be isolated from their daughter by the father. The fact
that it cost mother twice as much in gas money did not concern the

father. Therefore, financial abuse was a part of the coercive control tactics as well.

By now, you may realize that coercive control tactics do not occur separately. You may feel emotional abuse, isolation, and financial abuse combined within a given situation. You may identify male privilege connected with isolation, and intimidation or threats and coercion. Go ahead and bring all the different types of coercive control involved in an incident or series of incidents into your Transformational Journaling™. This will help you resolve the multiple impacts of coercive control tactics more easily.

Debra A. Wingfield, Ed.D.

Reality Check #16—**The Prickly Porcupine Co-Parent (Using Spiritual Abuse)**

Using Spiritual Abuse Coercive Control Tactics

Spiritual Abuse involves attitudes and beliefs that interfere with or keep you from practicing your religion or spiritual beliefs, or imposing the abuser's beliefs on you and requiring you to follow his belief system. The abuser places himself in the position of being the all-knowing one in your life. He may even challenge your understanding of God and put himself above God as being omnipotent or godlike. These attitudes and beliefs are meant as a form of mind control to coerce you into blindly following his lead.

Case examples of the coercive control tactic pattern—Using Spiritual Abuse

In one case, a woman adopted a fundamentalist practice of her religion. She met a man who was raised in the fundamentalist religious group, and they were married. They chose to raise their children in the fundamentalist religious group the husband belonged to, and their children understood the customs and practice of their religion from that point of view.

When the marriage became abusive, the mother decided to leave and took the children with her. She intended to raise the children in the fundamentalist religious community of the father. However, she was ostracized for leaving him, and the fundamentalist community closed ranks around her ex.

Her ex filed for change of custody because he did not believe his ex-wife was raising the children correctly based on his religious beliefs. The elders in the community supported him by testifying in court. Without any actual evidence, the court gave the abusive father sole legal and physical custody of the children. This father used his religion to remove the children from their protective mother and control their religious beliefs.

Let us look at spiritual abuse from the other end of the continuum. One husband and wife did not actively affiliate with a church, attend church, or engage in any religious or spiritual practices in their home. The husband and wife each had been raised in different religions, and never made a clear choice about religion or introduced their children to any specific religious practices. However, the mother did honor her Native American spiritual beliefs and shared that with her husband.

The couple separated. Following their divorce, the father was given primary parenting time with their child. Religion was a non-issue for the child during her pre-school and early elementary school years. Mother continued to share her Native American beliefs and brought those into her home with her children. Although the father did not support the mother in her practices, he discouraged their child from using those practices in his home.

During one weekend parenting time with mother, their child asked to attend religious services with her siblings and grandparents. This was acceptable to the mother. However, father was outraged that mother would allow this without consulting him first "since he was the primary parent." Instead of encouraging their child's curiosity about religion, the father refused to allow the child to attend any religious services or activities until the child "is old enough to make her own decision."

This type of spiritual abuse denies the child exposure to religious and spiritual beliefs. Additionally, this child will not have exposure to religion, which would allow her to make an informed choice when she is old enough to make her own decision. She will miss out on a part of her developmental process that can instill moral and ethical values as well as a foundation in a belief system that may be similar or different from the belief systems of her parents.

This is just one example of how abusers use "spiritual abuse" within their relationships or after their relationships end. This type of abuse is based on the abuser's desire to maintain spiritual control of the children.

Take a few minutes to review and assess how spiritual abuse may have been used during your relationship or may be going on since you left your abuser. Remember, you may have other types of spiritual abuse that is not part of the assessment. You can use your Transformational Journaling™ Focus Points™ to describe those after you complete the assessment.

If you prefer to print out the assessments so you can circle your responses, go to HouseOfPeacePubs.com and click on the Interpersonal Violence Assessments link to respond to the assessments. You will use what you discover with your Focus Points™.

Using Spiritual Abuse

1 __never, 2 __hardly ever, 3 __sometimes, 4 __often, 5 __quite often, 8 __not applicable, 9 __prefer not to answer

In the relationship	After you separated/ divorced	Spiritual Abuse
1 2 3 4 5 6 7	1 2 3 4 5 6 7	1. Your ex used your religious or spiritual beliefs to manipulate and control you.[5]
1 2 3 4 5 6 7	1 2 3 4 5 6 7	2. Your ex ridiculed your religious or spiritual beliefs.[5]
1 2 3 4 5 6 7	1 2 3 4 5 6 7	3. Your ex prevented you from practicing your religious or spiritual beliefs.[5]
1 2 3 4 5 6 7	1 2 3 4 5 6 7	4. Your ex forced your children to be reared in a faith that you did not agreed to.[5]
1 2 3 4 5 6 7	1 2 3 4 5 6 7	5. Your ex kept the children from attending any religious/spiritual groups.[5]
1 2 3 4 5 6 7	1 2 3 4 5 6 7	6. Your ex undermined relationships with people connected to your religious/ spiritual community.[5]
1 2 3 4 5 6 7	1 2 3 4 5 6 7	7. Your ex did not allow you to attend religious/spiritual activities outside attendance at organized services where you are limited to group prayer/ participation.[5]
1 2 3 4 5 6 7	1 2 3 4 5 6 7	8. Your ex cited scripture to justify abusive, dominating, or oppressive behavior.[51]
1 2 3 4 5 6 7	1 2 3 4 5 6 7	9. Your ex forced you to violate your religious beliefs.[51]
1 2 3 4 5 6 7	1 2 3 4 5 6 7	10. Your ex denied you the freedom to practice the religion of your choice. [51]
1 2 3 4 5 6 7	1 2 3 4 5 6 7	11. Your ex made oppressive demands based on his interpretation of scriptures or other religious teachings (e.g., "the scriptures say that you need to obey me because you are my wife").[51]

1 2 3 4 5 6 7	1 2 3 4 5 6 7	12. Your ex instilled religious guilt in you for not doing what he wanted you to do (e.g., "How can you call yourself religious if you don't forgive me?").[51]
1 2 3 4 5 6 7	1 2 3 4 5 6 7	13. Your ex's sense of marital entitlement causes him to justify his sexual demands, including forced sex (i.e., marital rape).[51]
1 2 3 4 5 6 7	1 2 3 4 5 6 7	14. Your ex involved or forced your children to witness ritual abuse (e.g., sacrificing pets).[51]
1 2 3 4 5 6 7	1 2 3 4 5 6 7	15. Your ex shamed or belittled your religious practices.[51]
1 2 3 4 5 6 7	1 2 3 4 5 6 7	16. Your ex manipulated others in your religious communities to control and ostracize you.[51]

How does he do that?

Some spiritual abusers are dogmatic about their religious beliefs and refuse to accept any interpretation of "their bible" except their own. Other spiritual abusers are just as dogmatic about *not* being involved in any religion or spiritual practice. They may say they are "against organized religion" or "anti-religion." They may say they believe in God, but are unable to express what that means to them. If your spiritual beliefs are outside what is traditionally accepted in society, spiritual abusers will use that to argue you are weird or mentally unstable.

A spiritual abuser may put down your religious or spiritual beliefs, background, or practices as meaningless or not strict enough, compared to his own beliefs. He may refuse to allow you to practice your beliefs in your home when you are together, or he may refuse to allow you to share your religious and spiritual beliefs with your children.

Alternatively, he may dictate what you can and cannot teach your children after divorce. He may misquote or use religious writings to his advantage regarding the relationship between men and women. He may mock your faith, sabotage or limit your faith practices, or misuse religious texts to justify his abusive actions or demands.

If he comes from a fundamentalist background or has any standing in your religious community, he may use that as a way to control you. He may say he knows what is "right" because of his status in the religious community. He may place himself as the one and only authority in your home that is knowledgeable about your religion and say that you have to do what he says and how he says to be a religious person.

If he chooses not to be involved in religion or any spiritual practice, he may make fun of your spiritual practices or your belief system. You may find yourself dropping your spiritual practices or only observing them in private, either when he is not home or in secret. Ultimately, if this happens, he is controlling your spiritual life.

Now it is time for you to use your Transformational Journaling™ Focus Points™ to identify the patterns of spiritual abuse used in by your abusive ex.

Focus Point™: What patterns of spiritual abuse do you see that are similar between what happened while you were in the relationship and what is happening since you left the relationship?

This Focus Point™ is for you to journal on how to approach the abusive parent in the future related to the specific coercive control tactic—Using Spiritual Abuse.

Focus Point™: Identify where in your life your ex is able to trigger you to respond to his demands just as he did in your relationship.

These Focus Points™ are for your journaling on how to approach the abusive parent in the future related to the specific coercive control tactic—Spiritual Abuse.

Focus Point: Identify where in your life your ex is able to trigger you to respond to his demands just as he did in your relationship.

Focus Point: Determine how you want to set up healthy boundaries to protect yourself in the future from being abused through "Spiritual Abuse."

Examples of how other protective mothers approach an abusive father with the specific coercive control tactic pattern—Using Spiritual Abuse

Protective mothers find a variety of ways to include spirituality in their home lives with their children. Those who are involved with organized religious groups continue their involvement and include their children in these activities. Other protective mothers who experienced restricted access to religious or spiritual activities teach their children about their spiritual/religious roots at home. They may teach them songs specific to their traditions. They may include holiday celebrations and activities in their homes. Most importantly, protective mothers involve their children with their religious and spiritual backgrounds in their homes and communities.

In one case, a mother who knew of her Native American roots shared what she knew with her children. She took a further step to find her tribe through genealogical research. Once she established these roots, she contacted the tribe and enrolled herself and her children. This step enabled this mother to obtain scholarships to attend college, and she helped her children do the same. This step towards developing a spiritual identity for herself and the children also provided her children with the grounding that comes from knowing they are welcomed into the tribe. Their spiritual practice now includes their Native American practices along with their religious practices.

Up to this point, you have assessed a number of coercive control tactics that occur prior to the end of the relationship and after separation/divorce. The previous coercive control tactics are considered non-physical abuse. They still have a major impact on the person being abused. They can result in long-term emotional impacts when they remain unresolved. When you use the Transformational Journaling™ Focus Points™, you have tools to help resolve the emotional impacts of non-physical abuse. Now, we turn our attention to other types of coercive control tactics identified specifically with the Family Courts.

Section III

Control Freak Tactics in Family Court
Stop your voice from being Silenced... Again

Many years of protective mothers' experience in the Family Court taught them that they could not expect fair, unbiased treatment. It is important to protect yourself and your children when making decisions about your children in the Family Court process. Although what you want is not ideal, it may be the one way you are able to maintain parenting time with your children. This enables you to teach your children how to protect themselves when you are unable to be present.

Debra A. Wingfield, Ed.D.

Reality Check #17-- **The Slippery Weasel Co-Parent (Using Litigation Abuse)**

Overview of the coercive control tactic pattern-Using Litigation Abuse

"Using Litigation Abuse" is the use of all phases of the legal process in family court to delay, extend, manipulate, and coerce a protective mother into complying with the abuser's demands. The purpose of Litigation Abuse may be to punish, take revenge on, or keep the protective mother from revealing the extent of the abuser's abusive behaviors during the relationship. The abuser floods the protective mother with legal paperwork (Paper Abuse) after she leaves and continues to overwhelm her with words on paper when he no longer has access to the protective mother to lecture her directly. These lectures often end with threats to take her back to court if she does not agree to his demands.

In addition to being abused by the abuser, protective mothers may be abused by attorneys they interview to take their case. For example, the first attorney one protective mother interviewed asked, "Why did you have more children with your husband if you knew he was abusive?" This not only shows the attorney's lack of understanding of coercive control tactics; it was, also, abusive to criticize her while she was asking for legal help.

Her next attorney told this protective mother, "Domestic violence abusers don't file for divorce." Obviously, this attorney did not understand that the husband's motivation was not to get a divorce; it was to get custody of their children. Before this protective mother went to her first court hearing, she fired this attorney. Additionally, this attorney was being bullied by the husband's attorney to immediately agree to a custody evaluation without allowing for due process according to the law. This is a violation of the mother's rights.

Here are some questions to ask an attorney during your first interview before you pay a retainer fee.

1. How many divorce cases have you handled?
2. How many of those cases were you able to settle out of court?
3. Do you practice Collaborative Divorce?
4. Do you know my spouse?
5. Do you know my spouse's attorney?
6. Are you familiar with local Family Court judges and how they rule?
7. Do you believe it is better to mediate and negotiate than go to trial?
8. Do you have experience negotiating child support, spousal support, large financial settlements, or business valuation? Ask specific questions about issues you think will come up during your divorce.
9. How many cases with complicated property settlements have you handled?
10. What was the outcome of those cases?

Questions about how your case will be handled:

1. Will you or another attorney in the firm be handling my case?
2. Can I meet anyone else who will be involved in handling my case?

3. What experience does he/she have?
4. Are you available via phone or email?
5. How would I reach you in an emergency situation after hours/on weekends?
6. Do you have a heavy caseload? Will you have time to devote to my case?
7. If I need to reach you, what is the best time of day?
8. Will I receive copies of documents filed with the court, all communication with my spouse's attorney and any other documents related to my case?
9. Will I be kept informed of all developments in my case?
10. Will you ask my opinion before planning strategy?
11. What are your personal feelings about spousal support?
12. What are your personal feelings about joint custody versus sole custody?

Questions about fees:

1. What is your retainer fee?
2. What is your hourly billing rate?
3. Do any fees I pay include the services of any associates who work on my case?
4. If my case goes to divorce court, will there be extra fees?
5. Will I sign a contract outlining the fee arrangement?
6. Will I be sent itemized bills?
7. Will I be kept updated about how the retainer fee is used and when it is used up?
8. Will you petition the court for my spouse to pay my attorney fees?
9. How much do you charge for letters and phone calls to my spouse's attorney or me?
10. How much will you charge for copies of all relevant documents?
11. Will there be other costs such as court filing fees, process server fees, or other extraordinary fees? Are

these costs included in your fees or do I pay them separately?

12. Will I be billed for communication via phone or email? If so what is your billing structure? Find out exactly how much the attorney charges and how he/she bills for his/her time.

Once you have interviewed and decided which attorney you want to hire, have that attorney draw up a fee contract. Do not give the attorney a retainer fee until a contract is written and signed by both you and the attorney. If the attorney refuses to do this, find another attorney.

Case examples of the coercive control tactic pattern—Using Litigation Abuse

Several cases have similar features when it comes to litigation abuse. Repeatedly, I hear from protective mothers that their attorneys discourage them from bringing up domestic violence, the abuser's coercive controlling behaviors, or abuse directed at their children. This is extremely frustrating for protective mothers because this is the reason that they leave the relationship and file for separation or divorce, and custody of the children. They understand that leaving the relationship may be the most dangerous and potentially lethal time for them, however, their overriding concern is protecting their children from witnessing domestic violence being perpetrated on them or the children being abused.

When their attorneys do not present these facts in the courtroom, protective mothers do not feel the court record accurately reflects their concerns for their safety as well as those of their children. Attorneys tend to minimize or diminish reports of domestic violence, coercive control, and child abuse directed at the couple's children, because their experience in court has shown them that these factors tend to backfire on the protective mother. The result is that often the abuser is given either shared custody or sole custody of the children.

While this is definitely not in the best interest of the children, the attorneys understand that judges have been educated and trained to have a bias against protective mothers. From a counterintuitive standpoint, attempts to explain this strategy to protective mothers can actually work against them. Until there is a reversal of this type of training and education, it is important for attorneys to explain the damage that may occur by bringing out these issues in a divorce proceeding.

Here is an example of Litigation Abuse that one frustrated protective mother shared with me in an e-mail:

"After meeting with my atty yesterday, I learned that the mess up in my case is irreversible. My ex-atty did not present in court, on the record, my ex-husband's IRA savings, retirement that we had accumulated during the marriage. He also did not show all of the income tax returns, nor subpoena [her ex-husbands'] latest. Neither did he show a credit card statement that showed [her ex-husbands'] ability to pay over $6,000.00 in one month to cover personal expenses.

By law here it's too late. That stuff had it's chance to be discovered and discussed. Now I'm 2 months behind on rent and nothing more is coming in.

My new atty said he doesn't understand why this info wasn't presented. He said he's going to look into it some more, but I may be pushed to sue my ex-atty for messing up. I hate suing people, but if it means I have to [do] this in order to put a roof over my kid's heads and feed them, then I'll have to sue. My atty will call me back when he returns from [a trip] and has some answers for me."

When co-parenting with an abuser is required by the court, protective mothers must learn how to create safe boundaries for themselves and their children while being forced to continue to interact with the abuser. Some of the difficulties that arise from this type of arrangement include exchanges, especially where children are reluctant to go with the abusive father. Fathers can use this to create additional litigation and make accusations that mothers are not encouraging their children to be involved with their other parent.

Protective mothers report being held in contempt of court for their children's refusal to go with their father. Protective mothers are jailed for their children's reluctance to participate in visits with their abusive parent. Mothers are forced to take part in therapy to learn how to force their children to agree to visit or engage in parenting time with their abusive parent.

In addition to the emotional toll this takes on the children, the mother is faced with the financial responsibility to pay for therapy. In some cases, judges reverse custody, giving the fathers sole legal and physical custody of the children, and requiring mothers to have supervised visits. This adds another level of financial abuse to the mother, who must pay for the supervised visits.

Along with payment for visits, mothers are ordered to pay child support. Numerous mothers have indicated that their child support payments are unreasonable for the amount of income they receive. Oftentimes, these child support orders are amended, without hearings, and the mother becomes so far behind in child support payments that her ex will take her back to court. She may end up jailed, fined, and unable to see her children because her ex threatens to have her arrested for non-payment of child support.

Take a few minutes to assess whether "Litigation Abuse" is/was used to control you. If you prefer to print out the assessments so you can circle your responses, go to HouseOfPeacePubs.com and click on the Interpersonal Violence Assessments link to respond to the assessments. You will use what you discover with your Focus Points™.

Using Litigation Abuse

1 __never, 2 __hardly ever, 3 __sometimes, 4 __often, 5 __quite often, 6 __not applicable, 7 __prefer not to answer

After you separated/ divorced	Litigation Abuse
1 2 3 4 5 6 7	1. Your attorney did not bring out in court evidence you provided to prove domestic violence/abuse or child abuse occurred during your relationship. [5]
1 2 3 4 5 6 7	2. Your attorney told you not to bring up the domestic violence that happened during your relationship because you did not report it to police and no arrest or court records of the abuse exist. [5]
1 2 3 4 5 6 7	3. Your attorney told you not to bring up how your ex abused the children or continues to abuse them because Child Protective Services refused to investigate or came back with an unfounded or unsubstantiated determination. [5]
1 2 3 4 5 6 7	4. Your ex or your ex's attorney responded to your one-page motion with huge amounts of court-related paperwork. [5, 45]
1 2 3 4 5 6 7	5. Your career was ruined because you missed appointments and deadlines to attend court hearings. [6]
1 2 3 4 5 6 7	6. After the separation, your ex's attorney contacted your children's therapist to have the two of you meet together with the therapist to discuss your children. [5]
1 2 3 4 5 6 7	7. Your court orders were prepared by your ex's attorney and contained many untrue statements. [5]

1 2 3 4 5 6 7	8. After your ex was court-ordered to pay you a substantial sum of money, he refused to pay anything. Your ex told the judge he would rather go to jail.[6]
1 2 3 4 5 6 7	9. Your ex used your request to increase child support as an opportunity to investigate your life, build a good enough case, refused to return the children after their summer visits, and used his substantial and respectable professional practice to gain permanent custody.[6]
1 2 3 4 5 6 7	10. Your ex got a restraining order prohibiting you from leaving the state with the children.[6]
1 2 3 4 5 6 7	11. Your ex married his girlfriend just before the court hearing, then talked in court about how the stepmother would be a stable influence on the children.[6]
1 2 3 4 5 6 7	12. Your ex arranged for his mother or new wife to care for your children even when you were available to do so. He used this arrangement in court to gain primary parenting time or sole custody (physical and legal).[5]
1 2 3 4 5 6 7	13. Your Attorney quit or withdrew from your case the day before or the day of the court hearing leaving you to represent yourself (Pro Se).[5]
1 2 3 4 5 6 7	14. Immediately after you separated and took the children with you, your husband/partner filed for emergency custody of the children claiming you were emotionally/mentally unstable.[5]

How does he do that?

Your ex is an accomplished liar and makes up all types of allegations about you when he talks with his attorney. He appears cool, calm, and collected to his attorney and may even engage in "good ol' boy" behaviors with male attorneys to convince them that they both think the same way about women. In fact, he looks for an attorney who will side with him and agree how you misunderstood him during the marriage. His focus is on how you never took care of him or his needs, your neglect of the children, and how he is the better parent and therefore needs to have sole legal and sole physical custody of the children. (Note: In some states the term "custody" is being changed to "parenting time" or "parental responsibilities"). In my experience, this is a common set of lies abusers use to gain sympathy from their attorney.

He takes advantage of reasonable choices you make, such as asking him to care for the children while you are experiencing temporary health problems, or moving to be close to family. He files for change of custody and receives it based on false allegations, lies, and statements that he swears to without any evidence to back them up. When you file an appeal and get the case remanded back to the court where the erroneous decision was made, the judge continues to rule in his favor, stating that the child is now settled with your ex and enrolled in school where your ex lives.

Another litigation ploy is to engage you in lengthy evaluations with court-appointed personnel to prove you are not able to take care of your children competently. This is in direct opposition to what was occurring during your marriage or relationship when he left the primary caretaking to you. When you were married, he claimed when he was caring for the children, he was "babysitting," not having responsible parenting time with them. Using court-appointed personnel is discussed in the following chapter. However, it is important to note that bringing multiple court-appointed personnel into your case usually leads to further financial abuse because you are expected to pay for one-half of their fees.

Now, it is time for you to go back through your assessment and review the areas of "Litigation Abuse" you determined are occurring in your co-parenting relationship.

How to respond to the coercive control tactic—Using Litigation Abuse

Identify the patterns that have occurred since you separated or after you received final orders and your ex decided to take you back to court. Use your Focus Points™ to describe what is happening now.

Focus Point™: What new patterns do you see your ex using since he does not have direct physical access to you?

Focus Point™: How is your ex using Litigation Abuse patterns as a co-parent?

Now, look at how you are triggered to respond in ways you previously used with this type of abuse.

Focus Point™: Identify where in your life your ex is able to trigger you to respond to his demands just as he did in your relationship.

This Focus Point™ is for your journaling on how you choose to approach the abusive parent in the future related to the specific coercive control tactic—Litigation Abuse.

Focus Point™: Determine how you want to set up healthy boundaries to protect yourself in the future from being abused through "Using Litigation Abuse."

Examples of how other protective parents approach an abusive parent with the specific coercive control tactic pattern—Using Litigation Abuse

Many times protective mothers look for attorneys to represent them without determining whether that attorney will be able to stand up to the attorney their partner chooses. This is the first area where protective mothers get off on the wrong track in Family

Court. Be sure to ask someone to help you find an aggressive attorney who supports mothers. Some of the interview questions discussed earlier can be very helpful.

Many changes are happening in the Family Courts about how divorce and/or custody cases are handled. The attorney who will stand up for you, and require your partner's attorney to negotiate as many parts of settlement and custody/parenting time as possible before you see the judge, will serve you better over the long-term. Work with an attorney who refuses to allow forced custody evaluations unless you agree they are necessary.

Your attorney is there to help you work with a delicate balance between what is best for your children and what the court will agree to support. One way to protect yourself and your children is to avoid going to court. If you have a strong attorney who knows what the judges are looking for in stipulated agreements, you may be able to work out most or all of your divorce or separation and custody/parenting time without going to court. Judges like this because they are overloaded with cases to hear. Be sure you are not coerced into making agreements that are harmful to you or your children.

One mother I worked with was pushed by her attorney and her ex's attorney to agree to unreasonable therapy following a psychological evaluation that was paid for by her ex. The psychologist labeled her with several mental health diagnoses that were not substantiated by her longtime psychiatrist who she saw for eight years prior to the custody dispute. The judge refused to believe the psychiatrist over the psychologist, who only saw this mother for a short time. We will come back to the issue of buying "court-related personnel" in the next chapter.

It should be noted here that this mother went to the psychiatrist due to concerns over severe panic attacks. Within three weeks of her first meeting with the psychiatrist, the medications she was prescribed were effective in controlling her symptoms. The lengthy time in treatment was the ongoing follow-up with the psychiatrist, which is normal in these situations. At no time, before or after she gave birth, was she a danger to her daughter. If a divorce did not happen, this mother would have continued to be the primary caregiver for their daughter. Being under the care of a medical doctor is not a reason to lose custody/parenting time with your children.

Keep in mind that your attorney is working for you. You are paying for your attorney's services. If you are not satisfied your attorney is representing you well, you can fire your attorney and hire someone else. One place to check out an attorney you are considering hiring is http://www.martindale.com/. When I help protective mothers locate attorneys, I check here first for someone in her area. I read the comments and reviews about each attorney and their practice focus. If possible, ask friends who have been through a divorce or custody case if they know how a prospective attorney handles cases.

You are putting your life and your children's lives in the hands of this attorney. Be sure you feel comfortable with the attorney you hire. An attorney who is a family friend or someone you know through church or another organization may not be the best choice unless you know he or she will aggressively work for you. You are divorcing an abuser and you know how cunning, convincing, conning, and charming abusers can be while at the same time they are lying and getting away with it. Protect yourself with the best attorney you can afford.

Reality Check #18-- **The Lying Rat Co-Parent (Using Court-Appointed Professionals)**

Overview of the coercive control tactic pattern-Using Court–Appointed Professionals

Using Court-Appointed Professionals involves added professionals in the custody or parenting time process. These professionals are used to humiliate, intimidate, and deny the parental qualities of the protective mother after separation that were acceptable prior to separation. By inserting court-appointed professionals in the custody process, the abuser/father gains the opportunity to portray himself as a "good enough" parent.

Help! Who are all these people meddling in our lives? Vultures at Work

The court may use many different professionals in custody/parenting time cases. These may be parenting assessors or evaluators, custody/parenting responsibility evaluators, child family investigators, guardians' ad-litem (GAL) or Child Legal Representatives (CLR), parenting coordinators, and mediators. Depending on the state in which you live, these people may have other titles as well.

Their indicated role in your case is to help the court determine what type of parenting arrangement would be in the "best interests" of your children. However, very often, these professionals lack in-depth training in domestic violence or coercive control tactics and they can make serious errors in their recommendations to the judge. Therefore, it is extremely important that you ask them about their expertise before you agree to pay for their services.

Here are some questions for you and your attorney to ask before agreeing for a professional to be involved in your case.

Key Questions to ask court-appointed professionals/therapists/psychiatrists and others when coercive control tactics are being used in your relationship

1.   How many hours of training do you have in Coercive Control Tactics in relationships?
      a.   Look for a minimum of 7-14 hours.
2.   How many hours of training do you have in Dynamics of Domestic Violence in Relationships?
      a.   Look for a minimum of 14-28 hours
3.   How many hours of training do you have on the Effects of Domestic Violence on Children?
      a.   Did that include long-term emotional and physical impacts?
      b.   Look for a minimum of 7-14 hours
4.   What is your understanding of the use of children as leverage by an abusive parent in high conflict/contested custody cases?
      a.   Watch out for use of terms like parental alienation, parental alienation syndrome, or similar terms. These are "red flags" this person does not understand Coercive Control Tactics.
Professionals need training in all these areas.

If you are required to go to therapy for yourself or for reunification of your children with their abusive parent, or your children are required to go to therapy, add these questions to the ones above.

5. When parents are no longer living together, how do you work with both parents around issues concerning their children?

6. How do you approach financial abuse of one parent by the other parent in therapy when the child is the client/patient? For example, one parent pays, but the other parent brings in the child and refuses to allow the other parent access to what is talked about in therapy or access to the therapist.

    a. Is the parent who brings the child to therapy responsible for paying for part or all of the therapy?

    b. Are both parents equally responsible for payment for therapy?

7. What is your approach to working with children's emotional, social, and cognitive development in shared parenting situations where prior Domestic Violence or Coercive Control Tactics are witnessed by a child?

    a. Look out for therapists who are more interested in reunification of a child who does not want contact with the other parent than meeting the emotional needs of the child.

    b. How willing is the therapist to explore, work with, and understand why a child does not want contact with one parent?

Protective mothers often find that court-appointed professionals listen differently to them than to their spouses/partners by holding them to a higher standard of care and responsibility for their children. In many cases, mothers talk about being interviewed for a much longer time period by the GAL/CLR, the Child and Family Investigator, or Parental Responsibility Evaluator/Custody Evaluator than the father. The reports that come from these court-appointed professionals tend to be biased toward the father, giving him much more leeway to make parenting errors. It is as if the father has not had major responsibilities for the children, but now that he does he is not required to show the same level of responsibility as the mother.

Another issue that mothers continually bring to my attention is alienation. Mothers are held responsible for the father's behavior. His being uninvolved, harsh, or referring to the mother negatively when the children do not want to spend time with him are seen as the mother's fault. The father blames the mother, through the court-appointed professional, and recommendations are made to limit mother's time with the children or even require supervised visits.

The truth is that the father is creating the circumstances where the children do not want to be connected with him. When the father does not comply with court orders, he is backed up by court-appointed professionals and the mother becomes the target of his blame. The father is not held accountable and the mother is punished. Sometimes the mother is punished by being held in contempt of court and being required to pay fines or pay the father's legal fees. Other ways mothers are punished are loss of primary parenting time, loss of joint legal or physical custody. In some cases, mothers are restricted to supervised visits or jailed.

Mothers and their children are sent to "reunification therapy" to improve the relationship between the children and the father. Courts often require mothers to force the children to see the father and spend time with him even if his actions and behaviors are causing the children to avoid parenting time with him. Because the blame is placed on the mother, she is required to pay for the therapy and the father is not responsible for any of the costs.

Mothers who listen to their children's concerns about their fathers and attempt to protect the children from the father's abuse or neglect share with me their children's reactions to forced parenting time with their fathers. Younger children, who are abused physically or sexually by their fathers, may experience multiple problems. These may show up as nightmares or night terrors, unwillingness to see their father in a supervised setting, or begging their mother not to make them go with daddy.

Older children have refused to see their father and either hide when he arrives for his parenting time or leave their home to hide with their friends. In one case, their father so negatively impacted two teenage boys when he took them to his home, they refused to see him except in a public location. When the father insisted the boys come to his home, where the father's girlfriend encourages the father to abuse the boys, the older boy told a counselor that he wanted to kill his father and commit suicide. This resulted in the boy's hospitalization. The father reacted by threatening the younger boy, through his school counselor, to force him to come for parenting time. This boy became physically sick and was picked up from school. He, then, refused to go back to that school. Eventually, the mother helped this boy decide to return to the school he was attending.

Court-appointed professionals are more interested in parents' rights than in children's responses to their parents. They refuse to learn and understand that these children are responding to the abuse and violence they were exposed to that led to the dissolution of the parent-child relationship. Court-appointed personnel are often focused on forcing relationships that do not work, and the ultimate price is the long-term impacts on the children. The questions above are provided for you to ask court-appointed therapists/counselors if you are required by the court to involve your children with their services.

A judge may assign a Guardian ad Litem (GAL) or Child's Legal Representative (CLR), Court-Appointed Special Advocate (CASA) volunteer, or other professional to represent your children's interests in court. Working with this person may present some difficulties if he or she does not have adequate training in domestic violence dynamics or coercive control tactics. An abuser can easily manipulate the professional to see you as the parent who would interfere in the abuser's relationship with the children.

Children often report these professionals do not accurately represent their wishes to the court. In fact, they may actually tell the court the opposite of what your children have requested. Children end up feeling disappointed and betrayed by these adults who are introduced to them as their "representative" to the court.

Here are some areas to question when a Guardian ad Litem or similar type of representative is appointed in your case:

Although the qualifications, responsibilities and processes revolving around the private guardian ad litem are similar in many ways to those of other types of guardian ad litem, there are distinct and specific statutory differences and requirements. These special instructions are provided to interested persons to enable them to understand the full scope of the qualifications and responsibilities. These requirements are an example of what is required in South Carolina (ChildLaw.sc.edu/frmPublications/SC%20BAR%20GAL%20 Guidelines.pdf).

Statutory Requirements for Guardians *ad Litem* in Private Custody and Visitation Cases (State of South Carolina)

Note to reader: Look for similar requirements or regulations in your state.

§ 20-7-1545 Private Guardians *ad Litem*

Guardians' *ad litem* are appointed by court order in private action before the family court in which custody or visitation of a minor child is an issue only when the court determines that:

(1) without a guardian *ad litem,* the court will likely not be fully informed about the facts of the case, and there is a substantial dispute which necessitates a guardian *ad litem*; or

(2) both parties consent to the appointment of a guardian *ad litem* who is approved by the court.

The court has absolute discretion in determining who will be appointed as a guardian *ad litem* in each case.

§ 20-7-1547 Qualifications

A guardian *ad litem* may be either an attorney or a layperson and must have the following qualifications:

(1) must be 25 years of age or older.

(2) must possess a high school diploma or its equivalent.

(3) an attorney guardian *ad litem* must annually complete a minimum of six hours of family law continuing legal education credit in the areas of custody and visitation; however, this requirement may be waived by the court.

(4) for initial qualification, a lay guardian *ad litem* must have completed a minimum of nine hours of continuing education in

the areas of custody and visitation and three hours of continuing education related to substantive law and procedure in family court. The courses must be approved by the Supreme Court Commission on Continuing Legal Education and Specialization.

(5) a lay guardian *ad litem* must observe three contested custody merits hearings prior to serving as a guardian *ad litem*. The lay guardian must maintain a certificate showing that observation of these hearings has been completed. This certificate, which shall be on a form approved by Court Administration, shall state the names of the cases, the dates and the judges involved and shall be attested to by the respective judge.

(6) lay guardians' *ad litem* must annually complete six hours of continuing education courses in the areas of custody and visitation.

(7) must not have been convicted of any crime listed: Offenses Against the Person; Offenses Against Morality and Decency;

Criminal Domestic Violence; Narcotics and Controlled Substances; or convicted of the crime of contributing to the delinquency of a minor.

(8) must not have ever been on the Department of Social Services Central Registry of Abuse and Neglect.

(9) Upon appointment to a case, a guardian *ad litem* must provide an affidavit to the court and to the parties attesting to compliance with the statutory

qualifications. The affidavit must include, but is not limited to, the following:

(i) a statement affirming that the guardian *ad litem* has

completed the training

requirements; (ii) a statement affirming that the guardian *ad litem* has complied with the requirements of this section, including a statement that the person has not been convicted of a crime;

and

(iii) a statement affirming that the guardian *ad litem* is not nor has ever been on the Department of Social Services Central Registry of Child Abuse and Neglect.

Appointment of an Attorney for the Lay Guardian

A party or the guardian *ad litem* may petition the court by motion for the appointment of an attorney for the guardian *ad litem*. This appointment may be by consent order. The order appointing the attorney must set forth the reasons for the appointment and must establish a method for compensating the attorney.

§ 20-7-1549 Responsibilities and Duties

The responsibilities and duties of a guardian *ad litem* include, but are not limited to:

(1) representing the best interest of the child.

(2) conducting an independent, balanced and impartial investigation to determine the facts relevant to the situation of the child and the family. An investigation must include, but is not limited to:

(i) obtaining and reviewing relevant documents, except that a guardian *ad litem* must not be compensated for reviewing documents related solely to financial matters not relevant to the suitability of the parents as to custody, visitation or child support. The guardian *ad litem* shall have access to the child's school records

and medical records. The guardian *ad litem* may petition the family court for the medical records of the parties.

(ii) meeting with and observing the child on at least one occasion.

(iii) visiting the home settings if deemed appropriate.

(iv) interviewing parents, caregivers, school officials, law enforcement and others with knowledge relevant to the case.

(v) obtaining the criminal history of each party when determined necessary.

(vi) considering the wishes of the child, if appropriate.

(3) advocating for the child's best interest by making specific and clear suggestions,

when necessary, for evaluation, services and treatment for the child and the child's

family. Evaluations or other services suggested by the guardian *ad litem* must not be ordered by the court, except upon proper approval by the court or by consent of the

parties.

(4) attending all court hearings related to custody and visitation issues, except when attendance is excused by the court or the absence is stipulated by both parties. A guardian must not be compensated for attending a hearing related solely to a financial matter if the matter is not relevant to the suitability of the parents as to custody, visitation or child support. The

guardian must provide accurate, current information directly to the court, and that information must be relevant to matters pending before the court.

(5) maintaining a complete file, including notes. A guardian's notes are his work product and are not subject to subpoena.

(6) presenting to the court and all parties clear and comprehensive written reports including, but not limited to, a final written report regarding the child's best interest. The final written report may contain conclusions based upon the facts contained in the report.

The final written report must be submitted to the court and all parties no later than 20 days prior to the merits hearing, unless that time period is modified by the court, but in no event later than 10 days prior to the merits hearing. The 10-day requirement for the submission of the final written report may only be waived by mutual consent of both parties. The final written report must not include a recommendation concerning which party should be awarded custody, nor may the guardian *ad litem* make a recommendation as to the issue of custody at the merits hearing unless requested by the court for reasons specifically set forth on the record. The guardian *ad litem* is subject to cross-examination on the facts and conclusions contained in the final written report. The final written report must include the names, addresses and telephone numbers of those interviewed during the investigation.

(7) A guardian *ad litem* may submit briefs, memoranda, affidavits or other documents on behalf of the child. A guardian *ad litem* may also submit affidavits at the temporary hearing. Any report or recommendation of a guardian *ad litem* must be submitted in a manner consistent with the Rules of Evidence in the state law.

§ 20-7-1551 Guardian *ad Litem* as Mediator

A guardian *ad litem* must not mediate, attempt to mediate or act as a mediator in a case to which he has been appointed. However, nothing in this section shall prohibit a guardian *ad litem* from participating in a mediation or a settlement conference with the consent of the parties.

§ 20-7-1553 Compensation

At the time of appointment of a guardian *ad litem*, the family court judge must set forth the method and rate of compensation for the guardian *ad litem*, including an initial authorization of a fee based on the facts of the case. If the guardian *ad litem* determines that it is necessary to exceed the fee initially authorized by the judge, the guardian must provide notice to both parties and obtain the judge's written authorization or the consent of both parties to charge more than the initially authorized fee. A guardian appointed by the court is entitled to reasonable compensation, subject to the review and approval of the court. In determining the reasonableness of the fees and costs, the court must take into account:

(1) the complexity of the issues before the court;

(2) the contentiousness of the litigation;

(3) the time expended by the guardian;

(4) the expenses reasonably incurred by the guardian;

(5) the financial ability of each party to pay fees and costs; and

(6) any other factors the court considers necessary.

The guardian *ad litem* must submit an itemized billing statement of hours, expenses, costs and fees to the parties and their attorneys pursuant to a schedule as directed by the court.

At any time during the action, a party may petition the court to review the reasonableness of the fees and costs submitted by the guardian *ad litem* or the attorney for the guardian *ad litem*.

§ 20-7-1555 Disclosure

When a guardian *ad litem* is appointed, he or she must provide written disclosure to each party of the nature, duration and extent of any relationship the guardian *ad litem* or any member of the guardian's immediate family residing in the guardian's household has with any party. He or she must also disclose any interest adverse to any party or attorney that might cause the impartiality of the guardian *ad litem* to be challenged and any membership or participation in any organization related to child abuse, domestic violence or drug and alcohol abuse.

§ 20-7-1557 Removal of the Guardian *ad Litem*

A guardian *ad litem* may be removed from a case at the discretion of the court

Parenting Coordinator

"Parenting coordination is designed to help parents implement and comply with court orders or parenting plans, to make timely decisions in a manner consistent with children's developmental and psychological needs, to reduce the amount of damaging conflict between caretaking adults to which children are exposed, and to diminish the pattern of unnecessary relitigation about child-related issues."

If a Parenting Coordinator is under consideration or appointed to your case, recognize there are many pitfalls for you. Liz Richards from National Alliance for Family Court Justice (http://nafcj.net) is an excellent resource for many issues in child custody where domestic violence, coercive control tactics, and abuse occur. She has a long list of reasons why you want to object strenuously to a Parenting Coordinator being assigned to your case. This additional person inserted into your life can create more problems rather than solve them. Essentially, a Parenting Coordinator takes over your decision-making responsibilities for any major decisions about your child. For example, these decisions may be in the areas of education, religious matters, or elective medical procedures.

Mediator

Most states have a law that requires divorcing or separating couples to go to mediation prior to going before a judge. Additionally, most states have provisions that make exceptions when domestic violence has occurred. These exceptions include every possible situation -- from the "victim of domestic violence" being required to mediate in the same room with the "abuser," to the use of separate rooms where the mediator moves between each person, to mediation being omitted from the case process.

It is important for you to remember that you can decline to be involved in mediation. Your ability to decline may depend on your ability to provide evidence of domestic violence or a pattern of coercive control throughout the relationship. Various forms of evidence that are considered include temporary or permanent restraining orders, reports from law enforcement of arrest for and conviction of the abuser for domestic violence, pictures taken of bruises and injuries, or hospital reports verifying injuries. These are just some examples of evidence that may sway a mediator to suspend mediation.

Some mediators may allow you to bring someone else in the mediation session with you, while other mediators will not.

Some mediators will only allow you to meet with them and refuse to allow an attorney, advocate, or close family supporter to be with you. You may be restricted to talking alone with the mediator even if you are not in the same room with your ex or soon-to-be ex. During breaks, while the mediator talks with your ex or soon-to-be ex, you may be able to discuss your options with your attorney, advocate, or close family supporter. Every state has different rules for mediation, and every mediator works a little bit differently, so you need to ask about the rules and guidelines.

Some mediators always ask about domestic violence before mediation starts. They may have a questionnaire for you to complete to find out something about you and your relationship. If there is not a question about domestic violence or coercive control tactics on the questionnaire, add that information. Unfortunately, many mediators are not trained to understand domestic violence and coercive control tactics if there is no physical evidence, such as pictures of bruises or broken furniture. Mediators usually do not understand about coercive control tactics and the long-term emotional impacts of living with an abuser.

Use the assessments in the previous chapters in this book to show the patterns of coercive control tactics used against you in your relationship. You may want to make a short list of those tactics that happened "quite often" or "often" to add to your information you provide the mediator. Tell the mediator what you mean by "quite often" or "often" in terms of how many times a week or times a month your ex or soon-to-be ex used those behaviors.

Your goal is to show a long-term pattern of behaviors that were harmful to you and your children. Use your "Focus Points™" to describe what these patterns were and how they affected you and your children. If your children saw or heard the coercive control, describe how often this happened and what your children did for their own safety when this was happening. If your children tried to stop the coercive control and were yelled at, hit, or emotionally or physically hurt during the incidents, include this in your statement as well.

Here are some questions to ask the mediator before you agree to have him or her mediate your case if you are ordered to mediate before you see a judge.

1. Does the mediator have a law degree and family law practice experience, and is the mediator informed of divorce and parenting research?

2. Does the mediator have actual or real knowledge of the subject matter of your conflict, or the issues you need help with?

3. Does the mediator have multiple years of experience or experience with multiple cases?

4. Does the mediator wear other professional hats, or limit his or her work to dispute resolution of divorce and family law matters?

5. How does the mediator address "parental responsibilities" and "parenting time" when domestic violence/abuse or child abuse occurred in the relationship?

6. What type of training does the mediator have in the area of child abuse, including physical abuse, emotional abuse, sexual abuse, and physical and emotional neglect?

What do I mean by "actual or real" in question two and "multiple" in question three? Refer to the questions earlier in this chapter about specialized training in coercive control tactics, domestic violence dynamics, the effects of violence on children, and the long-term effects of domestic violence and coercive control on children. During your mediation experience required by the court, you may have felt victimized by the mediator (secondary victimization), or you may have experienced re-victimization by your soon-to-be ex or ex-partner. Here are some of the positive and negative feelings you may have felt during mediation. Complete this checklist to review and understand your emotional experiences.

During the Mediation Meeting, I Felt:

	1- Not at All	2-A little	3-Neutral	4-Some of the time	5-A lot
Safe					
Believed					
Defenseless					
Heard					
Ashamed					
Respected					
Helpless					
Cared for					
Disbelieved					
Cared about					
Ignored					
Distressed					
Comfortable					
Unheard					
Interrogated					
Confident					
Empowered					
Scared					
Intimidated					
Listened to					
Dismissed					

Blamed					
Powerful					
Threatened					
Supported					

Here are some Focus Points ™ to consider about how you felt in mediation. Take some time to do the checklist on the next page before you complete these Focus Point s ™.

Focus Point ™: What feelings were positive for you during mediation?

Focus Point ™: What feelings were negative for you during mediation?

Focus Point ™: What responses by the mediator helped you feel safe?

Focus Point ™: What responses by the mediator felt victimizing?

Now it is time for you to assess how the abuser used "Court–Appointed Professionals" to continue to coerce and control you during the court process. If you prefer to print out the assessments so you can circle your responses, go to HouseOfPeacePubs.com and click on the Interpersonal Violence Assessments link to respond to the assessments. You will use what you discover with your Focus Points™.

Using Court-appointed Professionals

1 __never, 2 __hardly ever, 3 __sometimes, 4 __often, 5 __quite often, 6 __not applicable, 7 __prefer not to answer

After you separated/divorced	Using Court-appointed Professionals
1 **2 3 4 5** 8 **9**	1. Your court appointed custody evaluator, mediator, or guardian-ad-Litem (GAL) misinterpreted information collected in their interviews. [5,6]
1 2 3 4 5 8 **9**	2. The mediator assigned to your case did not allow you to meet in a separate room from your ex after you reported domestic violence or abuse of you or your children during the relationship. [5, 16]
1 2 3 4 5 8 **9**	3. Court-appointed professionals denied reports of coercive control tactics, abuse, or violence during custody evaluations, mediation, or GAL meetings even when documentation was provided to the professional. [6, 16]
1 **2 3 4 5** 8 9	4. Your ex alleged parental alienation against you when he was the one brainwashing the children against you. [5,6,11]
1 **2 3 4 5** 8 9	5. There was more than one Child Family Investigator, or custody evaluator appointed to your case. [5]
1 2 3 4 5 8 9	6. Mediators, custody evaluators, or GALs recommended or encouraged joint custody (50/50 split) even when presented with evidence of coercive control tactics, abuse, or violence. [16]
1 2 3 4 5 8 9	7. You were asked directly by the mediator, custody evaluator, or GAL if there was a history of coercive control tactics, abuse, or violence during the relationship directed at you and/or your children. [16]
1 2 3 4 5 8 9	8. When you insisted on divorce, your ex had you examined by multiple psychiatrists or psychologists. [6]
1 2 3 4 5 8 9	9. During mediation, custody evaluations, or meetings with the GAL, your experiences of coercive control tactics, abuse, or violence were not considered a safety factor for your children even if your ex showed signs of "physical abuse" toward the children before the meetings. [16]

1 2 3 4 5 8 9	10. Psychiatrists said your self-esteem was too low for you to be a good parent. [6]
1 2 3 4 5 8 9	11. During mediation, custody evaluations, or meetings with the GAL, your experiences of coercive control tactics, abuse, or violence were not considered a safety factor for your children even if your ex showed signs of "emotional abuse" toward the children before the meetings. [16]
1 2 3 4 5 8 9	12. The Psychiatrist/psychologist said your career was bad for your children. [5, 6]
1 2 3 4 5 8 9	13. When you were not asked, you directly, you told the mediator, custody evaluator, or GAL there was a history of coercive control tactics, abuse, or violence during the relationship directed at you and/or the children. [16]
1 2 3 4 5 8 9	14. You were afraid to tell the mediator, custody evaluator, or GAL there was a history of coercive control tactics, abuse, or violence during the relationship directed at you or the children. [16]
1 2 3 4 5 8 9	15. When you told the mediator, custody evaluator, or GAL there was a history of coercive control tactics, abuse, or violence during the relationship directed at you and/or the children, they would ask the father to respond to the allegations and ask for admissible evidence. [16]
1 2 3 4 5 8 9	16. The GAL was "charmed" by your abusive ex and he was given custody/unsupervised access to your children.[5]
1 2 3 4 5 8 9	17. Mediator, custody evaluator, or GAL preferences occurred regardless of who wants custody or whether abuse against the mother happened. However, if sole or primary custody is to be awarded to either parent, the mediator, custody evaluator, or GAL preferred to give as much time with the father as possible (i.e., liberal visitation in the case of sole custody)—especially if the father requests such time. [16] .
1 2 3 4 5 8 9	18. Multiple parenting supervisors were appointed to supervise your parenting time while the other parent received no supervised parenting time. [13]

1 2 3 4 5 8 9	19. When you told the mediator, custody evaluator, or GAL there was a history of coercive control tactics, abuse, or violence during the relationship directed at you or the children, they would dismiss abuse reports without evidence or would say it no longer mattered since you were not in the relationship anymore. This was especially true for non-physical abuse toward you. [16]
1 2 3 4 5 8 9	20. The mediator, custody evaluator, or GAL criticized or punished you for attempting to protect your children in ways the mediator, custody evaluator, or GAL did not understand. [16]
1 2 3 4 5 8 9	21. If sole or primary custody was awarded, the mediator, custody evaluator, or GAL favored the parent who meets one or more of the following criteria: a) does not use substances, b) employed, c) promotes children's education, d) ensures basic needs are taken care of (hygiene, housing, food), or e) acts professionally during the meeting (e.g. he does not act aggressively). [16]

How does he do that?

In more than one case, protective mothers were ordered by the court to have multiple evaluations because the evaluator or the court did not like the results of the evaluation. This is because the evaluations showed the mother being competent and mentally stable. Use of multiple evaluators is abusive to the protective mother. She is constantly having to prove her mental stability and competence as a parent.

Inserting mental health professionals into the case to "teach the parents how to co-parent" does not take into account the dangerousness of this type of situation. Again, the protective mother is having to balance between working with the mental health professional and monitoring her physical and emotional safety. Mental health therapists who are uninformed or lack training in domestic violence dynamics and coercive control tactics can easily re-victimize the protective mother with denials of their experience during the relationship.

They may accept that the danger was there during the relationship and minimize it now that the relationship is ending. They fail to take into account the increased lethality that occurs when controlling relationships end. The research and statistical data support many lethal ends for protective mothers, their children, or both once the final orders are in place. These lethal situations occur daily across the U.S. and in other countries.

A final example of how Using Court-appointed Professionals is abusive to protective mothers is through reunification therapy. This is in direct response to discredited writings by Dr. Richard Gardner who proposed "parental alienation syndrome" or PAS. Repeatedly, I hear from protective mothers who are required to take part in reunification therapy to encourage their children to see their abusive parent. This forced therapy is the responsibility of the mother to pay for since she is blamed for the children not wanting to be connected with their father. Sadly, the father's own behavior and attitude toward his children is responsible for children being reluctant to maintain a relationship with him.

When children are placed in the custody of or primary parenting time with their father, sometimes by force, the father is the parent who engages in brainwashing the children against the mother. To date, I have not experienced a case where the father was required to take part in "reunification therapy" with his children to reconnect the children with the mother.

How to respond to the coercive control tactic—Using Court-Appointed Professionals

Of course, you may have other experiences than those in the

assessment. Go ahead and list those experiences and assess them using the same scale. Take some time to use the following Focus Points ™ to journal about what happened in your case.

Focus Point ™: What experiences did you have with Mediators, Custody Evaluators, or GALs that affected your custody/parenting time with your children?

How does your ex take advantage of court-appointed professional's attitudes and beliefs about coercive control, abuse, and violence?

Although it is contrary to what you would expect, court-appointed professionals often refuse to believe that coercive control, abuse, and violence occurred in your relationship. They may believe that it is no longer a concern since you are separated or divorced. Therefore, they tend to disregard any statements on your part that safety is still an issue for you or your children. However, we know that coercive control, abuse, and violence can increase after separation.

This type of belief system feels supportive to the abuser and he uses it to continue to manipulate the professionals to do what he wants. What does he really want? He wants to retaliate against you for leaving or take revenge against you for ways he believes you have harmed him. His greatest weapon is using your children to hurt you. He feels justified in doing this because he believes he has a "right" to his children. He sees them as property, just as he sees you as his property. Therefore, he believes he can do anything he wants with his "property." He may not even care if he is harming the children emotionally, physically, or sexually. He does not relate to them as separate human beings, just property.

He may see the children as his to control. He wants to control their thoughts, their beliefs, and their physical bodies. These are some ways coercive controlling fathers do this.

After you separated, your ex sought unapproved contact with the children or kept you from having contact. For example, he kidnapped the children, kept the children longer than allowed, and returned the children to you later than allowed. Your ex made the children believe that anything you do for them is done only to make *him* look bad.

Your ex brainwashed the children. For example, he constantly bad-mouthed you until the children began to believe him. Your ex would alternate kindness and abusiveness with the children to create a trauma-induced bond with the children. Your ex led the children to believe that their safety depended on remaining close with him.

After getting custody, your ex turned over primary care of your children to another person. For example, he remarried, had a live-in girlfriend, or had daily help from his or her mother to care for your children. Your ex blamed the divorce or separation on you, and made sure the children knew that the spiritual and emotional costs to everyone in the family were your fault. For example, showed the children extreme religious texts or videos stating that divorce is a sin, and that sinners go to hell; taught children that the woman's role is to keep the family together, no matter what.

Your ex coached, bribed, or pressured the children to lie about you in court. Your ex insisted on joint custody as a strategy to reduce his child or spousal support payments. Your ex questioned the children about visits as a way to gather information about you. For example, he demanded to know, in detail, what they did, who they visited, where they went, who they saw, what they drove. Your ex told your children to keep secrets from you about their health, their grades, or his bad behaviors that frightened the children or put them in danger.

How to respond to the coercive control tactic—Using Court-Appointed Professionals

First and foremost, you must realize and understand that you have choices in every area where court-appointed professionals are brought into your case. Be very clear with your attorney, if you have representation, that you will not willingly accept the appointment of anyone to your case without you being able to check their background and credentials, interview them, and determine if they have the training and experience to work with a complicated case such as yours. This provides you breathing room and stops your ex from backing you into a corner and controlling the court-appointed professional through money, lies, and manipulation.

For example, in one smaller community, the court usually used one custody evaluator to do all the evaluations. This person was known for having close relationships with family law attorneys who represented fathers, and those attorneys used the evaluator to recommend fathers be given custody. The evaluator disregarded or ignored mother's claims of domestic violence, patterns of coercive control tactics, and/or child abuse in reports. Many children suffered further abuse at the hands of abusive fathers or were taught to be abusive to their mothers.

This situation happens far too often in communities all across the country. Other court-appointed professionals may have close connections with judges who appoint them as GALs, reunification therapists, or mediators. One mother reported that the judge ordered her to go to counseling with her child and for the father to take the child to the same counselor. The mother's attorney intervened and asked the judge to send the parents to a counselor outside their immediate area where they would not have direct social contacts within the community. The judge chose to follow the direction of the mother's attorney to avoid showing favoritism because he was up for re-election.

In another case, a mother was told to take her children for reunification counseling to a counseling center that had previously refused to see her or the children. When the mother called the counseling center and spoke to the director about her concerns, her attorney received a letter stating the father's therapist read some articles that said "reunification counseling" could be too traumatic for the children. It was a misguided way for the counselor to remove the counseling center from the dispute because the counselor and the director of the counseling center did not want to go to court and testify. This was followed by "Litigation Abuse" from the father's attorney.

The father's attorney wrote to the mother's attorney and told him that the father would be having unsupervised parenting time with the children that weekend (for 48 hours) after the children repeatedly refused to see the father at the Family Visitation Center. Mother's attorney stood up to the father's attorney and stated that only supervised visitation at the Family Visitation Center would be acceptable. The mother's attorney wanted the visit to be video-taped in order to show the court the response of the children and their mother.

Mother complied with the visitation request and brought her children to the Family Visitation Center. The oldest child screamed and cried and refused to see her father. The younger child saw her father for 25 minutes before she stopped the visit. Afterwards, she told her mother she did not want to visit father again.

Mother, in this case, did everything she could to encourage the children to visit with their father. She went so far as to enter the visitation room with her children while the father was there. They refused to stay or refused to see him. All this was documented by the visitation center.

It is most important from the time you decide to leave your spouse/partner that you document everything that happens with your children. Document your children's behaviors, statements, and emotional reactions with the dates, times, and locations. Document any coercive control directed at you by your spouse/partner or ex in the same way. If you can, make recordings of your exchanges or communications, and make sure to keep a copy in a safe place. You will have these documents and recordings to support your statements about what happened to you or your children. Make sure you keep a copy of any documentation that you give to your attorney.

In one case, the mother's attorney lost important documentation that was on a cell phone. When she arrived in court, the attorney informed her the cell phone was lost. She did not have any way to recover the information on the cell phone.

Take some time to complete the following Focus Points™ about how your soon-to-be ex or ex is using Court-Appointed Professionals to continue coercive control tactics with you.

Focus Point ™: What new patterns do you see your ex using since he does not have direct physical access to you?

Focus Point™: How is your ex using the patterns as a co-parent?

These Focus points are for journaling by you on how to approach the abusive parent in the future related to the specific coercive control tactic—Using Court-Appointed Professionals.

Focus Point™: Identify where in your life your ex is able to trigger you to respond to his demands through court-appointed professionals just as he did in your relationship.

Focus Point™: Determine how you want to set up healthy boundaries to protect yourself in the future from being abused through "Using Court-Appointed Professionals."

Examples of how other protective parents approach an abusive parent with the specific coercive control tactic pattern—Using Court-Appointed Professionals

Stick with the facts as much as possible in meetings with court-appointed professionals. Whenever your emotions take over, you are viewed as weak and unstable. Therefore, you may not be seen as a "fit parent," while your spouse/partner may be seen as a "good enough" parent. It may be hard to keep your emotions in check. You will be judged on your ability to handle the stress of the courtroom, and the numerous meetings with professionals who are only interested in whether they think you can provide stability for your children.

What do you do with all those emotions that are boiling up inside you? Find a support system, an advocate through a victim services organization, or check the resources section in this book for people who understand what is happening to you. They may have other resources where they can refer you. They are not trying to pass you off to someone else to get you out of their hair. They know the best people to help you with your particular needs.

Protective mothers have formed support systems through the internet on social networking sites, blogs, and forums. Check out various groups to find out what is most helpful to you. Many of these resources have different purposes. They will help you at different points in your case. Some resources provide information to help you understand the court system. Other resources provide support. Still others are involved in activism to change the way the court system operates and bring all these people into your life who were never around when you were an intact family.

Now that you are dissolving your relationship, the judge asks court-appointed professionals to help make decisions about "the best interests of your children." You are probably asking why this is necessary since you and your spouse/partner did all that without them up to this point. These court-appointed professionals do not know you or your children. They do not know the focus of your conflicts in your relationship that led to your separation. Your responsibility is to paint the most accurate picture you can of how your family worked when it was intact. Then, you have to sit back and wait for them to judge you.

Some mothers have complained that the picture these professionals painted of them and their family to the judge was very different from the reality of their lives. Many protective mothers are astounded when they find that once they were considered a "good enough" mother and now they are required to attend parenting classes, counseling, and even joint therapy with the person they separated from for good reason.

One mother found her agreement to meet with the "children's therapist" one-on-one was translated by the GAL/CLR as her agreeing to meet with the therapist and her husband who she separated from after repeated threats to kill her. The mother contacted the therapist and told the therapist she would be glad to meet with the therapist without her husband present. The mother asked the therapist if she understood the danger both she and the mother would face if the father was allowed to be present in the same interview. The therapist did not know how to respond. This is typical of therapists who are untrained in coercive control tactics or domestic violence.

Another mother challenged the GAL/CLR in court when the GAL/CLR overstepped her responsibilities. The GAL/CLR immediately asked to be removed from the case to save herself from a legitimate complaint to the bar association. This mother did her research and learned what the GAL/CLR could and could not do in her role. It is very important that you be assertive in your case.

In mediation, another mother found that if she maintained focus on the facts and did not allow her ex or his attorney to bully her into being emotional, she could more easily negotiate for the outcome she knew was in the best interest of their child. This mother prepared herself for the mediation. She made sure to keep control of her emotions and not allow herself to be caught up in a conflict with the father.

When a parenting coordinator was assigned in another case, the mother and I talked about a strategy for her conversation with the parenting coordinator. She expressed all her anxiety to me. We talked about keeping her focus on her goal in the upcoming meeting. The parenting coordinator was supportive of this mother's efforts to comply with the court order and approved the mental health professional she wanted to see. The good opinion of the mental health professional by the parenting coordinator went a long way toward her support in this situation. Also, the mother maintaining her composure during the meeting with the parenting coordinator helped her to be seen as stable and competent enough to parent her child.

Use your Focus Points™ to help you plan your strategy with court-ordered professionals. Then, share your plan with your safe support system. In this way, you are on your way to having a better outcome. If you still have doubts about your strategy, you can contact my office at **questions@houseofpeacepubs.com**.

Reality Check #19-- **The Charging Rhinoceros Co-Parent (Using Family Court Judges)**

Overview of the coercive control tactic pattern-Using Family Court Judges

Using Family Court Judges involves attitudes and behaviors the abuser uses to: (1) encourage the court to believe lies about his former partner; (2) put his behaviors onto his former partner to make the former partner look as if she is attempting to interfere with his parental relationship with the children; and (3) manipulate the courts into thinking the abuser is the stable, responsible parent. The purpose behind the abuser's behavior may be to retaliate or take revenge on his former partner for leaving, and/or to have access to the children to instigate child abuse or continue child abuse, or to reduce the amount of child support he is required by law to pay.

In addition to the abuser's manipulation of the courts, the protective parent encounters a values clash between the Family Court, the juvenile court, and the domestic violence/civil court. Look at how this occurs when the protective parent is "caught between a rock and a hard place".

Protective mothers must know that the values and norms are different in Family Court from domestic violence/civil courts and from juvenile courts addressing child protection complaints. Because these three courts operate on three different sets of values, confusion is created for anyone who does not understand these values. If you are trained in one set of court values, then seek to transfer those values to another court system, you are doomed to failure.

Also, you must understand that one court's values may actually operate at cross purposes to another court's values. For example, we are educated in our society to report suspected child abuse to Child Protective Services or law enforcement. We do this with the understanding that this government office is assigned the responsibility to protect children from further abuse.

However, the values change when the context of the complaint is framed as part of a custody dispute. In that context, the credibility of the complainant is diminished and cases are closed or put at the lowest level of concern. Even if a child comes forward to a non-parental adult to reveal abuse, the child may not be taken seriously. If qualified credible professionals follow their mandatory reporting requirements, their affidavits and testimony are considered tainted by the court. Each case is not reviewed on its merits. The cases are viewed through a different values lens, and children often end up being forced to live with their abusive parent.

Now let us return to the third type of court. In the civil court where protection orders are ordered, the victim requesting the order faces a different set of values. Here the court is concerned for her safety, physical and emotional. The value rests on keeping one adult safe from abuse from their intimate partner. If children are involved, the state statutes may allow the victim temporary custody of the children and the abuser forfeits access. This is a temporary forfeiture that can be amended or dismissed.

If an intimate partner violence situation leads to separation or divorce and Family Court becomes involved, the values for legal decisions may, and most likely will, change. Without preparation for this values shift, protective mothers (primarily) often become confused, discouraged, and may lose faith in the judicial system. Fixing these three value systems has been the focus of research since the late 1990s.

The fact that nothing has changed makes me wonder who benefits from maintaining these three separate value systems. On the other hand, I can tell you who is harmed by this values clash: the children who depend on the systems put in place to protect them. It is beyond time for lawmakers and judges to take up this urgent issue and blend these three value systems when children are caught in the crossfire. If we are to grow past the social problems that beset every community in our country, we have to stop putting children at risk to appease adults who exercise entitlement over child well-being. A proposed answer is to develop a fourth set of values where the three courts intersect.

When children fall under the jurisdiction of the Family Court, they are at the mercy of those judges. Parental access is the value of these courts, and their rulings trump the juvenile courts efforts to protect children from their abusers. What does this mean? Family courts are so focused on children having both parents in their lives that documented abuse reports are ignored and children are often sent to live with their abuser.

Case examples of the coercive control tactic pattern—Using Family Court Judges

In the following case example, a nine-year-old girl was returned to the custody of her abusive father. Despite overwhelming evidence presented in testimony by noted experts in child sexual abuse, and revelations of sexual abuse by the child as early as age 4, the court ordered this girl, now age 9, back to the home of her abusive father.

In a carefully choreographed script by the abuser and his attorney, in collusion with the judge, the hearing originally scheduled in the community where the child lived with her father was moved at the last minute to another community approximately one hour away. Only when mother, daughter, and their attorneys arrived at the courthouse were they notified of the change of venue. Visitors at the courthouse were questioned about their state of residence with the message that the hearing was not being held there. No further information was provided in hopes of deterring anyone planning to provide court watch from attending the hearing.

The court exercised coercive control over this nine-year-old girl and her protective mother. Because the mother had refused to return her daughter to her custodial father at the end of her summer visit after she revealed continued sexual abuse by her father, the judge gave the father an unsupervised visit for the day. As a trauma-informed therapist, it is beyond my comprehension that a judge would send a nine-year-old girl, who has repeatedly reported severe and traumatizing abuse, to spend a day with her abuser. There is absolutely no reason this child should have been subjected to being unprotected and re-traumatized by her father. This is just another problem with the Family Court value of parental access overriding the need for child protection.

In this case, the father is not being held accountable for his abuse. He is not required to obtain treatment as a sex offender. Nobody is psychologically preparing this child to be in her abuser's powerful presence. Even in a supervised setting by family, he still has access to intimidate and threaten her. She is defenseless. He may suggest that she should recant her statements. Even worse, he can make valid threats about harms he has threatened in the past to family members or her if she continues to complain about the abuse.

This judge's decision was seriously emotionally abusive to this child. Putting this child in an unsafe and dangerous situation goes against all the research regarding bringing an abused child together with her abuser. The girl has her trust betrayed once more by an abusive judge colluding with the abuser forcing reunification at the cost of the child's mental and emotional health and well-being.

Expert witnesses were as astonished as the attorneys, the mother, and especially the daughter at the outcome of this two-day hearing. This brave child spoke up and bravely talked to the judge about the sexual abuse and sodomy she has experienced for years at the hands of her father. She confidently told her mother she knew she would be going home with her as they departed for lunch.

At the end of the hearing, after hearing the stunning verdict, this brave girl was requested to re-enter the courtroom by the judge so that he could tell her how proud he was of her. Moments later her mother was told her daughter had left with her ex-husband without being able to say goodbye. In a state of surreal shock, the group left the courthouse to report to all their supporters the horrendous injustice that occurred that day. Sadly, this is not an isolated case.

Many protective mothers leave courtrooms without the ability to protect their children from further abuse. These good enough, fit parents who are the primary caretakers of their children, find themselves being punished not only by their ex abuser, but also by the judges who they turn to in the Family Court system to help them protect their children.

In another case, the judge changed custody from mother to father based on the older children's desire to live with father. The children did not want to do chores requested by mother. They wanted to live with father because he took them boating and did other fun activities with them. The children, also, told the judge they were angry with mother and threatened to hurt her. The judge told the mother he was changing custody for her protection. The result is that the children viewed the mother as abandoning them.

These are just a few examples of cases where judges have colluded with the abuser to continue the abuse of the children. There are many different types of cases with different dynamics occurring in courtrooms daily. Your case may be very similar to the cases discussed above or there may be differences in your case and situation. Now it is time for you to assess the kinds of coercive control tactics used by abusers to manipulate Family Court judges. Remember, your case may be similar or different from those identified in the assessment. Take some time now to complete the assessment.

If you prefer to print out the assessments so you can circle your responses, go to HouseOfPeacePubs.com and click on the Interpersonal Violence Assessments link to respond to the assessments. You will use what you discover with your Focus Points™.

Using Court-appointed Professionals

1 __never, 2 __hardly ever, 3 __sometimes, 4 __often, 5 __quite often, 6 __not applicable, 7 __prefer not to answer

After you separated/ divorced	Using Family Court Judges
1 2 3 4 5 6 7	1. The judge ordered you to have visitation only at the father's discretion.[6]
1 2 3 4 5 6 7	2. The judge threatened dire consequences if you do not obey.[12]
1 2 3 4 5 6 7	3. The judge treated you with a father-like attitude, denial of protection, and treated your claims as lies.[12]
1 2 3 4 5 6 7	4. The judge kept you from moving away from the abuser and kept you from family and resources by threatening loss of custody if you relocate.[12]

1 2 3 4 5 6 7	5. The judge allowed himself or herself to be fooled by your abusive partner's charm.[5]
1 2 3 4 5 6 7	6. The judge charged you with contempt and jailed you for not providing a cell phone for your child, even though the child has access to other phones or communication methods to use to communicate with the other parent.[5]
1 2 3 4 5 6 7	7. The judge put you in jail for protecting your children from an abusive (sexually, physically, emotionally) father.[5]
1 2 3 4 5 6 7	8. The judge used the abuser's previous threats to take your children away from you, making this nightmare come true.[12]
1 2 3 4 5 6 7	9. The judge ordered you into "alienation therapy" to learn how to stop "alienating" the children from their father.[5]
1 2 3 4 5 6 7	10. You wanted to move away and were prevented from moving away with your children even if this would allow them to survive economically and psychologically.[5,6]
1 2 3 4 5 6 7	11. The judge refused to issue or enforce adequate child support, spousal maintenance, or alimony orders, and can reinforce this control.[12]
1 2 3 4 5 6 7	12. Your ex kidnapped your child and then became assaultive to others after you found him. Multiple people pressed charges, and your ex was arrested. He was released without bail, once the judge understood it was a "domestic matter."[6]
1 2 3 4 5 6 7	13. The judge viewed your unwillingness to consider joint custody with an ex-partner who had never been *formally* charged with abuse or domestic violence as unreasonable.[5]
1 2 3 4 5 6 7	14. The judge didn't know enough about domestic violence victims, and misread how you looked or acted in court. For example, the judge viewed your passive behavior and well-groomed appearance as evidence that the domestic violence did not really harm you; the judge viewed your emotional behavior and exhausted appearance as evidence that you were "too emotional," mentally ill, perhaps lied about the abuse, or were abusive yourself. [20]

1 2 **3 4 5 6 7**	15. The judge refused to grant or enforce restraining orders against your abusive partner.[5]
1 2 **3 4 5 6 7**	16. The judge was inclined to favor the calm, cooperative, controlled (and controlling) father over you, the distressed, anxious, and difficult mother.[5]
1 2 **3 4 5 6 7**	17. The judge refused to consider psychological damage to your children as "abuse" and failed to include the children in protective orders.[5]
1 2 **3 4 5 6 7**	18. The judge issued restraining orders to both your abusive partner and to you, indicating that the abuse was partially your fault.[5, 35]
1 2 **3 4 5 6 7**	19. The judge viewed counseling received by the abuser as a "cure," and with no evidence of recent domestic violence incidents, treated the abusive partner as a responsible and caring parent.[5]
1 2 **3 4 5 6 7**	20. The judge down-played the domestic violence in the relationship, or refused to consider the pattern of abuse over time.[5, 20]
1 2 **3 4 5 6 7**	21. The judge treated domestic violence charges against your abusive ex-partner and against you as equally real, even though your ex filed charges against you as an intimidation strategy after you separated. [5]
1 2 **3 4 5 6 7**	22. The judge acted like he or she couldn't believe your financially stable, well-educated ex-partner could be a violent or abusive man.[5]
1 2 **3 4 5 6 7**	23. The judge believed your social or career problems were your fault, instead of the result of domestic abuse. For example, the judge didn't understand that your abusive spouse isolated you from your family and friends; didn't understand that your abusive partner prevented you from working outside the home. [5]
1 2 **3 4 5 6 7**	24. The judge counted only documented incidents of domestic violence, required evidence of several domestic violence incidents, counted only recent incidents, or required a higher standard of proof.[35]
1 2 **3 4 5 6 7**	25. The judge held you, the mother, to a higher level of care for the children than the father.[35]

1 2 3 4 5 6 7	26. The judge expects you, the mother, to have a job and support your children even if their capable father is unemployed by choice.[5]
1 2 3 4 5 6 7	27. The judge cut off your testimony before you had placed all facts in evidence.[5]
1 2 3 4 5 6 7	28. The judge allowed your ex to complete his testimony uninterrupted.[5]
1 2 3 4 5 6 7	29. The judge did not follow due process requirements by making an audio, video, or written record of all court proceedings.[5]
1 2 3 4 5 6 7	30. The judge placed gag orders on you to keep you from raising allegations of abuse/neglect or judicial misconduct.[35]
1 2 3 4 5 6 7	31. The judge didn't understand that <u>your thinking and memory problems</u> when being questioned may be the result of being an abused spouse. For example, your inability to remember important details or events were instead judged to be indicators of immaturity or lying instead of a result of stress, trauma, or Battered Woman's Syndrome.[20]
1 2 3 4 5 6 7	32. The judge didn't understand that your avoidance, emotional numbing, and distraction are the result of being an abused spouse. For example, your unusual responses in court regarding the abuse were thought to be indicators of not caring or lying instead of a result of stress, trauma, or Battered Woman's Syndrome.[20]
1 2 3 4 5 6 7	33. The judge didn't understand that your anxiety and nervousness in court may be the result of being an abused spouse. For example, your fearfulness, irritability, crying, and inability to focus were instead judged to be indicators of immaturity, or mental instability instead of a result of stress, trauma, or Battered Woman's Syndrome.[20]

How does your ex take advantage of magistrates or judges attitudes and beliefs about coercive control, abuse, and violence?

Remember when I talked about the Four C's an abuser may use to hook you into a relationship with him? Well, he uses those Four C's to effectively take advantage of the biases and myths magistrates and judges have heard in society and in judges training. He comes across looking calm, reasonable, and stable in the courtroom while you are emotionally pleading for the court to protect your children from abuse. In this way, he is seen as the parent more able to handle the children because he keeps his emotions in check.

Another tactic he may use with the court is to say something like, "I am more than willing to have her see the children." He presents himself as the "friendly parent." Your goal of protecting your children from further abuse makes the court wary of your ability to support a relationship between the children and their father. Instead of supporting your protective stance, the court may be more interested in your children having access to both parents, even if the abuse is validated by neutral professionals. The abuser aligns with the court's goal and convinces the court that if the court grants him custody/primary parenting time, he will ensure that your children have both parents in their lives.

Unfortunately, what happens after he obtains custody or primary parenting time that may be exactly the opposite. Too many mothers are refused access to the children by their ex. If this happens to you, you have to document this over time before you can go back to court. Meanwhile, your ex may be brainwashing the children by telling them, "Your mother doesn't want to see you." The children will believe you are the one who is refusing to see them instead of their father preventing them from seeing you.

He may also accuse you of lying and making false allegations about the abuse directed toward you and the children. He is likely to present as more believable than you, and this fits the bias the judge already holds. We do know that only about 2% of mothers make false allegations about the other parent. However, research shows fathers make false allegations about 16% of the time. Judges do not want to hear this from experts because it destroys the myths they are taught.

These biased attitudes and beliefs often result in mothers being reduced to limited visitation with their children or being put on supervised visits that become their responsibility to pay for or they cannot see their children. This further supports the abuser in his maltreatment of the children. It often leads to brainwashing the children against the mother.

If the court orders a shared parenting arrangement of 50% time with each parent, the abuser may create many obstacles to interfere with this arrangement. For example, one mother was forced to move from one end of the state to the opposite end of the state in order to maintain the 50% time arrangement. The court was not interested in the fact that she owned her home and was stably employed, whereas her ex lived in a remodeled chicken coop and lived off his parents. Because the custody case was filed in the county where the father lived, the judge ordered the child to attend school where the father lived. Clearly, this was not in the best interest of the child.

In other cases, judges have changed custody/parenting time from a shared arrangement to a sole custody arrangement when the mother was out of town during his parenting time. The father claimed the mother abandoned the children and he should have sole custody of them. He, further, brainwashed the children to think their mother did not want them, and they began rebelling against her. When the mother returned to court, the judge told her that he was changing the custody arrangement because he was concerned the children might harm her. Eventually, this mother felt she could not get fair treatment in this court and moved away from the small community where other people there ostracized her.

Now that her children are all adults, she is having a difficult time re-establishing a bond with them. They believed all the lies their father told them. He died so he cannot be questioned about what she tells them that is the truth.

I have encountered numerous situations since working with protective mothers. Each has their own unique characteristics. However, there are themes that seem to flow through most of the situations. These include a father who is focused on retaliating against his ex for not staying with him. His retaliation comes in the form of gaining the court's favor for custody/primary parenting of the children. Once he gains this level of control, he begins to brainwash the children (if mothers do this, they are accused of alienation, a discredited scientific ploy of fathers to shift access to fathers) by saying negative things about the mother, degrading her to the children, and attempting to interfere with the mother-child bond.

In addition, there are many situations where the father abuses the children sexually, physically, emotionally, or through neglect. These abuses are denied, or forensic professional testimony is not considered by the court and mothers end up with further limits on their time with their children. Over time, the children may pull away from their mother in attempts to stop being abused or they develop Stockholm Syndrome to protect themselves from being caught in the middle. Sadly, judges are ordering mothers not to take their children to physicians or therapists to prevent mothers from having professionals report child abuse by the father.

This is very painful for mothers because they feel the loss and grief that comes with losing a child who is still alive but has rejected them. Many protective mothers I work with who have reached this point are using the Transformational Journaling™ tools to help them release their children to become adults. With their own work, these mothers are able to move forward with their lives and allow their children the space they need to grow into adults who have choices about coming back into relationship with their mothers.

At the same time, in my work with protective mothers, we continue to work toward resolution of the "Broken Family Court System." We are attempting to change the culture, attitudes, and beliefs of Family Court judges through carefully developed education and training about the dynamics of coercive control tactics. We are working to support the adult children who were forced by the courts to live with their abusers who are now speaking out about their lives. With a growing effort across the U.S. and internationally, the message is starting to seep through the bias and myths. We are pushing hard to make it a flood that will wash away the erroneous decisions that put children in harm's way with abusive fathers and build a child-centered court system that truly honors the rights of children.

How to respond to the coercive control tactic—Using Family Court Judges

Now, it is time for you to clearly pull together your situation and to look at how you want to address it. Use the following *Focus Points™* to journal about your court experiences and build your path to healing and wholeness for yourself and your children.

Focus Point™: What new patterns do you see your ex using since he does not have direct physical access to you?

Focus Point™: How is your ex Using Family Court Judges with coercive control tactic patterns as a co-parent?

These Focus points are for journaling by you on how to approach the abusive parent in the future related to the specific coercive control tactic

Focus Point™: Identify where in your court experiences your ex is able to trigger you to respond to his demands just as he did in your relationship.

Focus Point™: Determine how you want to set up healthy boundaries to protect yourself in the future from being abused through "Using Family Court Judges."

Examples of how other protective parents approach an abusive parent with the specific coercive control tactic pattern—Using Family Court Judges

Remember, once you enter the Family Court system, your case is under the court's jurisdiction until the youngest of your children has aged out of the system. What this means is the Family Court will be looking over your shoulder until your youngest child reaches the age of majority, either age 18 or 19, or a specific age identified in your state custody/parenting time laws. If you want to move to another state or even to another location in your state, the Family Court can say your children must stay in the county where your case was filed originally.

This is one reason why abusers will file for divorce and custody first. They want to have local judges in charge of your case. Then, if you get an outstanding job offer or just want to move closer to your family for their support, you have to get permission from the judge to move with your children. The judge may tell you that the children must remain in the county so if you decide to move, the judge will transfer sole custody to their father and put you on a visitation schedule. This type of coercive control is often used in litigation to keep you trapped where your abuser will be able to stalk you or keep you controlled.

In one case, the judge signed off on most of the mediated agreement between a protective mother and her ex, gave her ex custody, and put her on visitation with her daughter. She was required to pay child support to her ex based on minimum wage since she was self-employed and did not have a steady income. This mother was punished for not having a stable income after she had stayed at home to raise their daughter.

By the time of the court hearing, the mother was out of funds to pay her attorney and had to go to court *pro se* (representing herself). This mother's attorney knew she sold her house and all her furnishings except her daughter's bedroom set to pay the attorney fees. At the last possible moment and in the most crucial hearing, this woman's attorney abandoned her. This happens quite often, and the abuser is usually able to continue payment for his attorney since he has more resources than the mother. Not only did the mother lose her attorney to represent her, she was required by the judge to pay part of her ex's attorney fees because the judge thought she was taking advantage of the court's time by bringing her motion. However, when ex's use the same tactics, judges do not tend to penalize them in the same way or for the same reasons.

Debra A. Wingfield, Ed.D.

Section IV
Control Freak Tactics with Physical and Sexual Violence

Before and after separation the abuser may use physical and
sexual coercive control tactics with you. Just because you have
left the abuser, in his mind, you still belong to him. You were
his hostage, his property. Be sure to protect yourself physically
and sexually from the abuser after you are no longer in the
relationship. Otherwise, you may find yourself giving birth to
another child with him or he may interfere in future
relationships.

Debra A. Wingfield, Ed.D.

Reality Check #20--**The Stalking Fox Co-parent (Using Non-Physical Sexual Abuse)**

Overview of the coercive control tactic pattern-Using Non-physical Sexual Abuse

Using Non-physical Sexual Abuse involves attitudes and behaviors designed to control your sexuality within your relationship. A coercive controlling partner often expresses these attitudes by making comments about how you look, behave, and respond to your partner's questions and comments concerning your body and your sexuality. The purpose of non-physical sexual abuse is to maintain control over your body. This may include your appearance, your dress, and any sexual responses you may have.

Your partner may pick out all your clothes for you and decide which clothes you can wear in your home and which clothes you can wear outside your home. Your partner may make comments about your weight to indicate you need to lose or gain weight. Your partner may make comments about your body in reference to your breasts being too big or too small, your bottom being too large or too small, or show jealousy when you are nursing your baby and say to stop because he is the only one who should suck your breasts. Your partner may tell you how to wear your hair at home and in public or whether you should dye it or curl it. He may accompany you to the hair salon to tell the hairdresser how to cut your hair.

Case examples of the coercive control tactic pattern—Using Non-physical Sexual Abuse

One type of non-physical sexual abuse that some protective mothers have experienced is their ex's involvement with pornography. For example, one mother found porn books and magazines under the bed in her bedroom after her ex left the house. When she started moving his trunk outside so he could pick it up, she found more porn magazines. This might show up today on computers where porn sites are readily available to those who want to find them. This type of non-physical sexual abuse is a way for the man to show the woman that he does not feel he is receiving the kind of sexual intimacy he wants and is getting it somewhere else.

To add insult to injury, this mother discovered a number of checks her ex wrote at a strip club while they were still together. When she asked about these, he told her he went there with business associates because that is where they wanted to go to talk about business. She later found out that he was cashing checks at the strip club to buy drugs.

In other cases, women report being accused of having affairs when there is no possibility of that happening. The abuser monitors them so closely that there is no opportunity to engage in an affair. However, these women report after leaving the relationship finding evidence of their husband or former partner having affairs. This form of non-physical sexual abuse damages the woman's self-esteem and undermines her sense of self-worth.

You may have similar circumstances that occurred in your relationship. For example, her current husband accused one mother of having affairs or preferring to be with her ex-husband. He used this type of non-physical sexual abuse as a way to force his wife to prove she loved him by having sex with him. His verbal and emotional abuse as well as threats lead to her complying with his demands rather than continuing the other abuse. There is a huge difference between consensual sex and non-consensual or unwanted sex.

Assessment of the coercive control tactic pattern—Using Non-Physical Sexual Abuse

Take some time now to look over the types of non-physical sexual abuse. Assess whether any of these types of non-physical sexual abuse tactics occurred in your relationship. You may have other examples of non-physical sexual abuse that happened in your relationship. Be sure to bring those out in your Transformational Journaling™ Focus Points™.

If you prefer to print out the assessments so you can circle your responses, go to HouseOfPeacePubs.com and click on the Interpersonal Violence Assessments link to respond to the assessments. You will use what you discover with your Focus Points™.

Using Non-Physical Sexual Abuse

1 __never, 2 __hardly ever, 3 __sometimes, 4 __often, 5 __quite often, 6 __not applicable, 7 __prefer not to answer

In the relationship	After you separated/ divorced	Non-physical sexual abuse
1 2 3 4 5 6 7	1 2 3 4 5 6 7	1. Your abuser accidentally left "porn" sites or a love letter open on the computer.[1]

1 2 3 4 5 6 7	1 2 3 4 5 6 7	2. Your abuser forced you to have sex with strangers. while he watched.[2]
1 2 3 4 5 6 7	1 2 3 4 5 6 7	3. Your abuser made jokes about parts of your body.[3]
1 2 3 4 5 6 7	1 2 3 4 5 6 7	4. Your abuser told you how to wear your hair at home and in public, whether to change the color or wear it curled or straight.[5]
1 2 3 4 5 6 7	1 2 3 4 5 6 7	5. Your abuser forced you to watch sexually specific material.[4]
1 2 3 4 5 6 7	1 2 3 4 5 6 7	6. Your abuser engaged in humiliating sexual examinations, checking to see if you had sex with someone else.[2]
1 2 3 4 5 6 7	1 2 3 4 5 6 7	7. Your abuser engaged in bathroom inspections to make sure you are not in the bathroom too long.[2]
1 2 3 4 5 6 7	1 2 3 4 5 6 7	8. Your abuser forced you to use birth control or prevented you from using birth control in an attempt to get you pregnant so you would have to stay with him.[5] This is sometimes called "Reproductive Abuse."[43]
1 2 3 4 5 6 7	1 2 3 4 5 6 7	9. Your abuser photographed you nude or while having sex over your objections.[4]
1 2 3 4 5 6 7	1 2 3 4 5 6 7	10. Your abuser challenged you for having post-divorce sexual activity with someone else.[6]
1 2 3 4 5 6 7	1 2 3 4 5 6 7	11. Your abuser refused to make love to you for extended periods of time (months or years).[6]
1 2 3 4 5 6 7	1 2 3 4 5 6 7	12. Your abuser engaged in underwear inspections, making you remove your panties so he can visually see any indications of sexual activity; sniffing your panties to see if they have an odor indicating sexual activity.[5]

1 2 3 4 5 6 7	1 2 3 4 5 6 7	13. Your abuser forced you into a sexually limited marriage while he was openly involved sexually with others.[6]
1 2 3 4 5 6 7	1 2 3 4 5 6 7	14. Your abuser told you what clothing you could wear at home, only with him present, and how to dress when going out in public.[6]
1 2 3 4 5 6 7	1 2 3 4 5 6 7	15. Your abuser told you how to wear your make-up when in front of him and how to wear make-up in public.[6]
1 2 3 4 5 6 7	1 2 3 4 5 6 7	16. You felt starved for affection in your relationship.[6]

How does he do that?

Your abuser may make indirect comments about how you wear your clothes, what clothes you wear, or how you wear your hair. He does not say directly that you should do something differently with your clothes or hair. His comments are meant to make you feel uncomfortable with what you are choosing. Your abuser says it would be better for him to make those decisions for you. He may tell you he likes your hair color your natural color even if you want to change your hair color. He may suggest that you dye your hair to a color he prefers or suggest you use a color close to your natural color.

The message here is that he wants to be in charge of your body. It is important to remember that you have a right to choose how you dress, wear your hair, and whether you want to have body piercings or not. Your body is only under your control, and no one has a right to tell you anything different.

Another form of non-physical sexual abuse involves his controlling how, when, and where you may be photographed and who may photograph you. You do not have to "please" your partner by agreeing to let him take photos of you that you are not comfortable having taken. One teenage girl reported that she was asked by her father, who had been separated from her mother since she was age one, to take a nude picture of her mother for him. This girl was disgusted that her father would ask her to do this. Of course, she refused because she recognized his request as inappropriate.

How to respond to the coercive control tactic—Using Non-physical Sexual Abuse

Consider all the types of non-physical sexual abuse tactics in the assessment or others you have experienced since your separation to respond to the following Focus Points™.

Focus Point™: What new patterns do you see your ex using since he does not have direct physical access to you?

Focus Point™: How is your ex "Using Non-physical Sexual Abuse" patterns as a co-parent?

These Focus points are for journaling by you on how to approach the abusive parent in the future related to the specific coercive control tactic Non-physical Sexual Abuse.

Focus Point™: Identify where in your life your ex is able to trigger you to respond to his demands just as he did in your relationship.

Focus Point™: Determine how you want to set up healthy boundaries to protect yourself in the future from being abused through "Using Non-physical Sexual Abuse."

Examples of how other protective parents approach an abusive parent with the specific coercive control tactic pattern—Using Non-physical Sexual Abuse

After separation or divorce many parents consider whether to date, become involved in a committed relationship, or even remarry. A number of questions arise for the parent. However, a jealous co-parent may engage in non-physical sexual abuse by making comments about their former partner dating, bringing another person into the lives of their children, or even prohibiting their former partner from allowing another adult to enter the lives of their children. These prohibitions can come in the form of threats to obtain sole custody of the children, fabricating lies about you and making sure they get back to the person you are dating, or threats of inflicting serious harm on you if you allow the children to acknowledge your new partner as a step-parent. Children may be threatened not to call the step-parent "dad" or even talk about the step-parent with their father.

The ultimate goal of this type of coercive control tactic is to prevent you from having a satisfying adult relationship with someone of your choice. You may feel so threatened that you put aside any thoughts of an emotionally or sexually intimate relationship until all your children have aged out of the court system.

Some mothers find it best only to engage in emotional or sexual intimacy when their children are with the other parent. They start out dating without telling the children they have taken that step until they are sure the relationship is solid and is leading to a permanent commitment. This type of decision does not allow the children to gradually get acquainted with mother's new friend, while it protects them from having to meet repeated different potential partners who mother eventually rejects.

If a mother knows the father is continually questioning the children about her dating interests, she may decide it is best to keep those relationships quiet until she feels certain that the relationship has promise for a long-term commitment. By now, you are probably thinking, why do I have to put my life and happiness on hold while the father has either paraded a string of women through the children's lives or remarried? That is an excellent question.

First, as a caring parent who wants what is best for your children, you know it can be emotionally damaging for the children to meet multiple potential male partners before you feel committed. Second, you want to make sure the new person you introduce to your children is not an abuser. You do not want them having that experience repeated. Third, you may want to enjoy having male companionship without the commitment of remarriage. You have always put your children first, and in this arena, you do not want to make an exception.

How do you know if you are making a healthy choice with a new partner? This question comes up very often when women who have been abused begin to date again. Use the assessments in each chapter of this book to evaluate what you are experiencing with a potential partner. Take your time to get to know the person you are dating very well. Find out which states he has lived in, and check with local law enforcement in those states for any reports of abuse or domestic violence against him, even if they were not prosecuted for an offense.

One mother I worked with was contacted by a fiancée of her former boyfriend (her child's father) and asked about why she left him. After she shared the type of abuse her ex used with her, the fiancée disappeared from his life. You do not want to subject another woman to an abuser's behaviors if she openly asks for his history with you. You would appreciate knowing this if you were in her shoes.

Reality Check # 21-- **The Chest-Beating Gorilla Co-Parent (Using Physical Abuse/Violence)**

Overview of the coercive control tactic pattern-Using Physical Abuse/Violence

Physical abuse/violence was defined by Straus & Gelles in 1986 as "an act carried out with the intention, or perceived intention, of causing physical pain or injury to another person". This is behavior intended, at a minimum, to cause temporary physical pain to the victim. It includes relatively "minor" physical actions like slapping with an open hand up to severe acts of violence that lead to injury and/or death. It may occur just once or infrequently in a relationship, but in many relationships it is repetitive and chronic, and it escalates in frequency and severity over time. Physical abuse/violence is what most people think of as "domestic violence." By now, you know that physical abuse/violence is only one of many types of coercive control.

In cases going through the Family Court, there is often little to no physical violence. When it does occur, that can become the breaking point where a mother says to herself, "I am not going down this road. I am leaving the relationship and I am protecting my children from experiencing physical abuse/violence." Instead of filing a police report or finding a domestic violence shelter, the mother goes to Family Court expecting to get help to protect herself and her children from a long history of coercive control that has now escalated to physical violence.

Family Courts are unprepared to address physical violence and coercive control tactics, so the mother does not feel supported by her attorney, the judge, or any of the other court-appointed professionals. If she pushes the court too hard, she may experience a backlash. The backlash is the large number of cases where abusers get custody of the children and mothers end up with supervised visitation.

Recent research and professional publications are just starting to address these issues. If this is happening in your case, please see the resource section of this book for research to provide to your attorney immediately. Also, you can contact me at info@houseofpeacepubs.com and I can help you find supportive individuals you can connect with to help you with your case.

Case examples of the coercive control tactic pattern—Using Physical Abuse/Violence

One young mother who was attempting to leave a coercive controlling relationship shared with me that her boyfriend pushed her up against the wall ... but it was only once. I explained that this was an escalation from verbal, emotional, and mental coercive control to physical abuse/violence. It never occurred to her that her relationship reached that point because it was all so subtle over a period of years. Sadly, most victims of coercive control and violent abuse have accepted the view of the general public that domestic violence means being severely beaten up with visible bruises, and bloodied noses, busted lips, or broken bones.

Another mother, who went directly to Family Court to escape her abusive relationship, told me the first time her husband ever became physically abusive/ violent with her was when she was eight months pregnant. Her husband pinned her down on the bed, got on top of her, and attempted to strangle her. She was able to get away from him after some time and decided to leave when their baby was two weeks old. It is not uncommon for coercive control tactics to escalate to physical abuse/violence during pregnancy.

Physical abuse/violence is generally not the first type of coercive control a woman experiences. Escalation to this level of abuse may only happen after all the abuser's non-physical coercive control tactics are no longer working. Then, the underlying message from the abuser is, "I hurt you once and I will do it again if you don't bend to my non-violent coercive tactics." This is another reason women who look to the Family Courts are not seen as victims of domestic violence.

Take some time now to look over the types of physical abuse/violence. Assess whether any of these types of physical abuse/violence tactics occurred in your relationship. You may have other examples of physical abuse/violence that happened in your relationship. Be sure to bring those out in your Transformational Journaling™ Focus Points™.

If you prefer to print out the assessments so you can circle your responses, go to HouseOfPeacePubs.com and click on the Interpersonal Violence Assessments link to respond to the assessments. You will use what you discover with your Focus Points™.

Using Physical Abuse/violence

1 __never, 2 __hardly ever, 3 __sometimes, 4 __often, 5 __quite often, 6 __not applicable, 7 __prefer not to answer

In the relationship	After you separated/ divorced	Physical abuse/violence
1 2 3 4 5 6 7	1 2 3 4 5 6 7	1. Your ex spit at you.[3]
1 2 3 4 5 6 7	1 2 3 4 5 6 7	2. Your ex held your head under water in the toilet.[2]
1 2 3 4 5 6 7	1 2 3 4 5 6 7	3. Your ex denied you sleep.[2]
1 2 3 4 5 6 7	1 2 3 4 5 6 7	4. Your ex threw something at you.[3]
1 2 3 4 5 6 7	1 2 3 4 5 6 7	5. Your ex choked you, sometimes to unconsciousness. [3,6]
1 2 3 4 5 6 7	1 2 3 4 5 6 7	6. Your ex hit, kicked, or punched you.[3]
1 2 3 4 5 6 7	1 2 3 4 5 6 7	7. Your ex hit you or tried to hit you with something.[3]
1 2 3 4 5 6 7	1 2 3 4 5 6 7	8. Your ex threatened you with a knife, gun, or other weapon.[3]
1 2 3 4 5 6 7	1 2 3 4 5 6 7	9. Your ex pushed or grabbed you.[3]
1 2 3 4 5 6 7	1 2 3 4 5 6 7	10. Your ex pulled your hair.[3]
1 2 3 4 5 6 7	1 2 3 4 5 6 7	11. Your ex burned you with cigarettes.[2]
1 2 3 4 5 6 7	1 2 3 4 5 6 7	12. Your ex physically abused you after separation or divorce.[5]
1 2 3 4 5 6 7	1 2 3 4 5 6 7	13. Your ex beat you up for having an affair you did not have although your partner openly had extramarital affairs.[6]
1 2 3 4 5 6 7	1 2 3 4 5 6 7	14. Your ex prevented you from eating; only allowed you to eat at certain times; only allowed you to eat certain foods; forced you to eat foods you did not like or want.[4]
1 2 3 4 5 6 7	1 2 3 4 5 6 7	15. Your ex tried to block you from leaving.[3]

1 2 3 4 5 6 7	1 2 3 4 5 6 7	16. Your ex pinned you to the wall, floor, or bed.[3]
1 2 3 4 5 6 7	1 2 3 4 5 6 7	17. Your ex entered your home after you were divorced, told your date to leave, then punched you until you ended up in the hospital.[6]

How does he do that?

As you consider the coercive control tactics that involve physical abuse/ violence, remember that your ex still considers you his property. This means he may escalate to physical abuse/violence after you separate even if that never took place before you left. It is important to continue to be aware of what is happening around you when you are out in your community as well as when you are home.

Abusers have entered the home of their ex without invitation to attack them, beat them up, and in some cases, killed them. In other cases, anyone else who was in the home is subject to being physically assaulted or killed. It is up to you to make sure you and your children are safe.

Abusers who remarry and continue their physical abuse/violence with their new partner do not always keep their abuse focused on that person. Many mothers tell me that their remarried ex is still controlling their lives, in addition to controlling the lives of their new spouses. It is almost as if once a coercive controlling man has partnered with you, he considers you a partner for life. This can lead him to attack you physically even after a divorce or permanent separation. Since there are no boundaries in his mind, he is able to justify hurting you to get what he wants.

How to respond to the coercive control tactic—Using Physical Abuse/Violence

You may be tempted to skip over these focus points because you are no longer in an intimate relationship with your abuser. You will find it helpful to monitor your physical safety and that of your children by building your awareness of what physical abuse occurred in the past and what red flags may appear in the future.

Focus Point^{TM}: What new patterns do you see your ex using since he does not have direct physical access to you?

Focus Point^{TM}: How is your ex using the patterns as a co-parent?

These Focus points are for journaling by you on how to approach the abusive parent in the future related to the specific coercive control tactic physical abuse/violence.

Focus Point: Identify where in your life your ex is able to trigger you to respond to his demands just as he did in your relationship.

Focus Point: Determine how you want to set up healthy boundaries to protect yourself in the future from being abused through "Using Physical Abuse/Violence."

Examples of how other protective parents approach an abusive parent with the specific coercive control tactic pattern—Using Physical Abuse

We know from the fatality research that the most dangerous time for a woman leaving an abusive relationship is when she is leaving and/or when her ex realizes that he no longer can control her. Sometimes an abuser believes that as long as you are going through divorce or custody proceedings, there is still a chance that you will return to the relationship. Only when he knows you are gone for good may he escalate to lethal violence. Many mothers report that they still feel fearful of their ex many years after the relationship ends. It is helpful to know this so you do not think this is happening only to you.

The best way to keep yourself safe is to maintain your awareness of your surroundings. Be cautious about being followed, especially at night. Lock your car doors and your doors at home, even if you are at home, and even if you live in a safe neighborhood. If your ex decides to teach you a lesson by physically abusing you, he will just walk into your home if your doors are unlocked.

Have a safety plan and be prepared to use it. Know where you can drive for help in your neighborhood. A first choice would be the closest fire station or a law enforcement department office that is manned. Although it may sound strange, you should pull into an area designated off limits to the public. You will get immediate attention that way. Be prepared to follow whatever orders are given by law enforcement until you can explain your situation. Be safe and keep your children safe.

You may wonder why I included the above information in this book. It is so easy for prior victims of coercive control and abuse to get complacent about their situation once they leave their abuser. I want you to be safe and know the full extent of the dangers that can follow you after you leave your abuser.

Reality Check #22—**The Territorial Tiger Co-Parent (Using Physical Sexual Abuse)**

Overview of the coercive control tactic pattern-Using Physical Sexual Abuse

Sexual abuse involves attitudes and behaviors that are motivated by the abuser's feelings of entitlement and rights to be physically sexual with their partner or spouse whenever, however, and wherever they feel like it. Sometimes abusers show sexual respect to their committed relationship partner prior to marriage.

Sometimes, it is only after marriage abusers engage in sexual coercion and abuse. In an abuser's mind, sex is now his right and he is entitled to sex because he has a certificate of marriage. His interpretation of this certificate is that he now owns you, and your choices are no longer his concern.

As long as the marriage contract is in place, or you have committed to a monogamous relationship (only having sex with him), he shifts to an entitlement position where he asserts his possessiveness of you. The abuser no longer views you as a separate person with a separate identity. He now considers you his property to do with as he pleases. At this point, he demands sexual compliance, which he defines as consensual sex.

"Sexual compliance involves willing consent to unwanted sex despite a lack of sexual desire." "Compliance involves consenting to unwanted sexual penetration without sexual desire in the absence of immediate partner sexual pressure." When asked "why [do] women go along with sex that they do not want?" In the case of coercive controlled relationships, they talk about the following reasons: compliance due to the "partner's previous acts of sexual coercion"; it was easier than arguing; she "knew what would happen if she didn't agree"; "because she was afraid of what would happen if she didn't".

As is the case with many protective parents, she learned that sexual refusals might result in being pressured psychologically or physically into sex (i.e., sexual coercion). Sexual coercion is defined as "nonconsensual unwanted sex." This "involves surrender to immediate partner pressure."

Case examples of the coercive control tactic pattern—Using Physical Sexual Abuse

The first time I heard this from a protective mother, I was shocked because I could not imagine a husband treating his wife in this manner. Since I have been doing this work for many years, I am no longer shocked, just disgusted that some men believe they are entitled to control the women in their lives this way. Here is what I heard.

"When I wanted to buy a special sweater [could be any special item], my husband told me I would only be able to get the sweater if I had sex with him first. I knew he would not give me the money if I did not have sex with him. The sweater was very important since it was a warm ski sweater at a very good sale price. I agreed to have sex, but it left me feeling dirty and used. I know I never want to live with someone who treats me that way again."

Just a little side note: If you feel used, it won't be long before you can become *ab*used. Pay attention to your feelings and listen to that little voice inside that is telling you how to protect yourself.

When one protective mother decided to leave her husband, she informed him of her plan. He knew there was nothing he could do to stop her. One of his last requests of her was to have sex "one final time" with a strong underlying message that if she refused he would physically assault her. This mother complied because it was the easiest of his hurtful behaviors to endure. As I talked with her about this incident, I explained to her that this was "marital rape." She did not realize this until that point. It helped her put all her uncomfortable feelings about the incident into place. She now understood why this impacted her at such a deep emotional level.

Other women have shared various experiences of sexual abuse during their marriage as well as after separation. Women have talked about being forced to have sex after being physically beaten by their husband. They have had various objects inserted into their vagina causing serious pain and even physical injury that required surgery to repair. One woman told me her husband stuck a loaded gun in her vagina and as he straddled her body, he said, "All I have to do is pull the trigger and your brains will be splattered all over like a fine pink mist."

Take a few minutes to assess how your partner used sexual abuse in your relationship. Also, look at how your partner used sexual abuse after you left your relationship or forced you to come back to the relationship because he convinced you that you still loved him or you would not have had sex with him. Consider how your partner used sexual abuse in order to get what he wanted in your separation or divorce agreement.

If you prefer to print out the assessments so you can circle your responses, go to HouseOfPeacePubs.com and click on the Interpersonal Violence Assessments link to respond to the assessments. You will use what you discover with your Focus Points™.

Using Physical Sexual Abuse

1 __never, 2 __hardly ever, 3 __sometimes, 4 __often, 5 __quite often, 6 __not applicable, 7 __prefer not to answer

In the relationship	After you separated/ divorced	Sexual Abuse
1 2 3 4 5 6 7	1 2 3 4 5 6 7	1. Your ex required you to have sex in exchange for money, drugs, clothing, or other things.[4]
1 2 3 4 5 6 7	1 2 3 4 5 6 7	2. Your ex physically forced you to have sexual intercourse.[3]
1 2 3 4 5 6 7	1 2 3 4 5 6 7	3. Your ex pressured you to have sex after you said no.[3]
1 2 3 4 5 6 7	1 2 3 4 5 6 7	4. Your ex inflicted pain on you during sex.[3]
1 2 3 4 5 6 7	1 2 3 4 5 6 7	5. Your ex blamed you because others found you attractive.[3]
1 2 3 4 5 6 7	1 2 3 4 5 6 7	6. Your ex pressured you to have sex after a fight.[3]
1 2 3 4 5 6 7	1 2 3 4 5 6 7	7. Your ex pressured or forced you into other unwanted sexual acts (oral, anal, etc.).[3]
1 2 3 4 5 6 7	1 2 3 4 5 6 7	8. Your ex used weapons or other (non- sex related) objects during sex inside your vagina.[5]
1 2 3 4 5 6 7	1 2 3 4 5 6 7	9. Your ex told you it was your obligation or duty to have sex with him. [39,40,41,42]

1 2 3 4 5 6 7	1 2 3 4 5 6 7	10. Your ex had sex with you without giving you the opportunity to say "no." For example, he began to have sex with you while you were still asleep and continued against your will.[39,40,41,42]
1 2 3 4 5 6 7	1 2 3 4 5 6 7	11. Your ex treated you like a sex object, told you what to wear to excite him, said you only belonged to him and he could have sex with you whenever he wanted it.[3]
1 2 3 4 5 6 7	1 2 3 4 5 6 7	12. Your ex was insensitive to your sexual needs.[3]
1 2 3 4 5 6 7	1 2 3 4 5 6 7	13. Your ex made you incapable of saying "no" to sex by drugging you or spiking your drink. [39,40,41,42]

How does he do that?

There are many different ways your partner may have manipulated you through physical sexual abuse during your relationship. He may still feel he has physical sexual rights to you after your relationship has ended. He may make comments about how he misses having sex with you. On the other hand, he could suggest during exchanges that you have sex before he takes the children or after he returns them. He may go so far as to talk you into having sex with him. You comply because you feel unsafe to say no.

One mother experienced severe internal injuries to her reproductive organs because of the sexual abuse during her marriage. She required multiple surgeries to repair the damage. This is one of the most extreme cases I have encountered. Other mothers tell about having objects shoved up their vaginas.

Many mothers report they are forced to have sex with their

partners following a severe beating as his way of making up to her. She is not free to say no and can only attend to her wounds after he has finished with her. This is not consensual sex and is in no way connected to loving intimacy. This is "marital rape" or "relationship connected rape."

Other types of sexual abuse mothers experience can include grabbing and pinching of body parts, including breasts and buttocks, with the intention of inflicting pain. Abusers will justify this by saying, "I know you like it rough." If you protest, you may find yourself being physically abused for denying him his "right" to hurt you.

How to respond to the coercive control tactic—Using Physical Sexual Abuse

Again, you may think this section does not apply to you so why cover the Focus Points™? Some protective mothers I work with have endured long, stressful, and heart-wrenching court battles with their ex when he is sexually abusing the children. Take some time to use your Transformational Journal™ to carefully look at how your ex may be using physical sexual abuse with you or your children.

Focus Point: What new sexual abuse patterns do you see your ex using since he does not have direct physical access to you?

Sometimes abusers redirect their sexual abuse behaviors onto their children after their adult partner has left the relationship. When children report these behaviors in an attempt to get help, they often tell their non-offending parent first. Protective mothers are caught in a dilemma about reporting sexual abuse of their children. They are taught that they are to report to their local child protection agency or law enforcement. When they do this as the non-offending parent, the Family Court may see this as an attempt to interfere with the abusive parent's rights to equal access or more parenting time.

In too many of these cases, I have seen the court actually give sole legal and physical custody to the abusive parent and put the non-offending parent on supervised visits. Not only are the children of these mothers being sexually abused, but these mothers also are being abused by the Family Court for attempting to protect their children. When children continue to report being sexually abused by their custodial parent, documentation by professionals is being dismissed by the court. You may be asking how this is "sexually abusing the mother." Because, in essence, the abuser is saying, "If I can't have sex with you (the mother), I will have sex with our child as a substitute for you (the mother)." This is extremely distorted thinking and obviously very harmful to your child.

Focus Point: How is your ex using sexual abuse patterns as a co-parent?

These Focus points are for you to journal on your approach to the abusive parent in the future related to the specific coercive control tactic-Using Sexual Abuse.

Focus Point: Identify where in your life your ex is able to trigger you to respond to his demands just as he did in your relationship.

Focus Point: Determine how you want to set up healthy boundaries to protect yourself in the future from being abused through "Using Physical Sexual Abuse."

Examples of how other protective parents approach an abusive parent with the specific coercive control tactic pattern—Using Physical Sexual Abuse

Protective mothers who receive reports of sexual abuse by their children naming their father as the abuser ask me, "How do I protect my child when I do not have the ability to monitor them 24/7?" We focus on two main areas: "good touch, bad touch," and setting healthy boundaries. Depending on the age of the child, even young children can be taught about not letting someone touch their private parts. We call those parts by their clinical names: penis for boys, and vagina and breasts for girls. The easiest way to help children understand what their private parts are is to explain, "They are those parts covered by your swimming suit."

When we talk with children about setting healthy boundaries, we help them learn that they can say to an adult "stop touching my privates" or "my privates are off-limits." Next, we help them learn how to do their own toileting, bathing, and dressing so they are not dependent on either parent in this area.

Finally, we teach children that they can tell their protective parent or a safe other adult (teacher, counselor, school principal, or law enforcement officer) if they feel uncomfortable being around another adult or if they have been touched in their privates. We also teach children that if an adult does something to them they don't like, then says "it's our secret," it is necessary to tell a safe adult.

This is one of the most serious problems we run into in Family Court because myths are being perpetuated that protective mothers make "false allegations" of abuse to keep their children away from their fathers. The courts fail to consider that the non-offending parent is responding to their children's requests for safety. Instead, the courts punish the protective mother and the children by awarding sole legal and physical custody to the abuser. Once this takes place, abusers often use their powerful, court-endorsed position to prohibit the children from having contact or parenting time with their protective parent.

Protective mothers have developed multiple support systems to help them through the trauma of having their children removed from their lives. As this movement grows and becomes more organized across the U.S. and other countries, more pressure is being put on legislators to correct these issues. Some groups organize demonstrations locally as well as on the national level. Other groups provide emotional support through social media. A growing awareness is being brought to the general public about the abuse within the Family Courts. Ultimately, everyone involved is focused on protecting children from further harm by their abusive parent.

Debra A. Wingfield, Ed.D.

Appendix A:
References for Assessments

1. Stark, E. (2010). *Reframing child custody decisions in the context of coercive control.* In Domestic violence, abuse, and child custody: Legal strategies and policy issues. Hannah and Goldstein, (eds.). Civic Research Institute: Kingston, NJ.

2. Stark, E. (2007). *Coercive Control: The Entrapment of Women in Personal Life.* Oxford University Press: NY

3. Simmons, C. A., Lehmann, P, & Craun, S. W. *Women Arrested for IPV Offenses: Abuse Experiences Yet Low Trauma Pathology.* Journal of Family Violence Volume 23, Number 8 / November, 2008

4. Dutton, Mary Ann, Goodman, Lisa and Schmidt, R. James (2005). *Development and Validation of a Coercive Control Measure for Intimate Partner Violence.* COSMOS Corporation 3 Bethesda Metro Center, Suite 400 Bethesda, Maryland 20814 Prepared for: National Institute of Justice Office of Justice Programs U.S. Department of Justice 810 Seventh Street, NW Washington, DC 20531 retrieved from http://www.ncjrs.gov/pdffiles1/nij/grants/214438.pdf

5. Wingfield, D. (2011). Observed behavior or reported directly to author.

6. Chesler, P. (2011). Mothers on trial: The battle for children and custody. Lawrence Hill books: IL

7. Bancroft, L. (2004). When dad hurts mom: Helping your children heal the wounds of witnessing abuse. Berkley books: NY.

8. Bancroft, L. (2002). Why does he do that? Inside the minds of angry and controlling men. Berkley books: NY.

9. Bancroft, L. & Silverman, J. G. (2002). The Batterer as parent: Addressing the impact of domestic violence on family dynamics. Sage Publications, Inc.: CA.

10. Adams, A. E., Sullivan, C. M., Bybee, D., & Greeson, M. R. (2008). Development of the Scale of Economic Abuse, Violence Against Women, Vol. 14 no. 5 563-588

11. Fink, P. J. (2010). Parental Alienation Syndrome in Domestic violence, abuse, and child custody: Legal strategies and policy issues. Hannah and Goldstein, (eds.). Civic Research Institute: Kingston, NJ.

12. Brigner, M. (2010). *Why do judges do that?* in Domestic violence, abuse, and child custody: Legal strategies and policy issues. Hannah and Goldstein, (eds.). Civic Research Institute: Kingston, NJ.

13. Sutherland, T.J. (2004). *High Conflict Divorce or Stalking by Way of Family Court? The Empowerment of a Wealthy Abuser in Family Court Litigation: Linda v. Lyle - A Case Study.* Massachusetts Family Law Journal, 22(1&2) 4-16.

14. Zorza, Joan PPT © 2010 Joan Zorza, Esq. joan@zorza.net Mike Brigner, Esq. mike.brigner@sinclair.edu

15. Bancroft, Lundy (2007) *Checklist for Assessing Change in Men Who Abuse Women* http://www.lundybancroft.com/?page_id=254.

16.   Rivera, Echo A. (2010). *Safety concerns and conciliation experiences among women divorcing controlling or abusive husbands.* Masters of Arts Thesis, Michigan State University. Psychology

17.   AmericanBar.org/groups/probono_public_service/projects_awards/child_custody_adoption_pro_bono_project.html

18.   APA.org/practice/guidelines/parenting-coordination.pdf

19.   TheLizLibrary.org/site-index/site-index-frame.html#soulhttp://www.thelizlibrary.org/parenting-coordination/parenting-coordination.html

20.   Lenore E.A. Walker Ed.D. A.B.P.P., Dorothy M. Cummings L.C.S.W. and Nicholas A. Cummings Ph.D. Sc.D. (Eds.) (2012). *Our Broken Family Court System.* NY: Ithaca Press.

21.   Elizabeth, V.; Gavey, N., & Tolmie, J. (2012). *Gender through Custody Law "... He's Just Swapped His Fists for the System" The Governance of Gender through Custody Law.* Gender & Society 26: 239-260. originally published online 27 February 2012. http://gas.sagepub.com/content/26/2/239.full.pdf+html

22.   Elizabeth, V.; Gavey, N., & Tolmie, J. (2010). *Between a Rock and a Hard Place: Resident Mothers and the Moral Dilemmas they Face During Custody Disputes* Feminist Legal Studies, Volume 18, Number 3, December, pp. 253-274(22).

23.   Rivera, E. A., Sullivan, C. M., & Zeoli, April M. (2012). *Secondary Victimization of Abused Mothers by Family Court Mediators.* Feminist Criminology, vol. 7, no. 3, pgs. 234-252.

24.   Hardesty, J. L., & Chung, G. H. (2006). *Intimate partner violence, parental divorce, and child custody: Directions for intervention and future research.* Family Relations: Apr, 55, 2; pg. 200 - 210.

25.   Pilnik, L., JD, & Kendall, J. R., JD (2012). *Victimization and Trauma Experienced by Children and. Youth: Implications for Legal. Advocates*1. Child & Family Policy Associates. SafeStartCenter.org/pdf/issue-brief_7_courts.pdf

26.   Birnbaum, R. & Saini, M. (2012.) *A Qualitative Synthesis of Children's Participation in Custody Disputes,* Research on Social Work Practice July vol. 22 no. 4. Pgs. 400-409.

27.   Principal Investigator: Daniel G. Saunders, Ph.D., Co-Investigators: Kathleen C. Faller, Ph.D. and Richard M. Tolman, Ph.D. (October 31, 2011). *Child Custody Evaluators' Beliefs About Domestic Abuse Allegations: Their Relationship to Evaluator Demographics, Background, Domestic Violence Knowledge and Custody-Visitation Recommendations.* University of Michigan, School of Social Work, 1080 S. University Ave., Ann Arbor MI 48109-1106. ssw.umich.edu/about/profiles/saunddan/Custody-Evaluators-Beliefs-About-Domestic-Abuse-Allegations-Final-Tech-Report-to-NIJ-10-31-11.pdf

28.   Haselschwerdt, Hardesty, and Hans (2011). *Custody Evaluators' Beliefs About Domestic Violence Allegations During Divorce: Feminist And Family Violence Perspectives.* Journal of Interpersonal Violence, 26:1694.

29.   Pence, E., Davis, G., Beardslee, C., & Gamache, D. (June 2012). *Mind the Gap: Accounting for Domestic Abuse in Child Custody Evaluations,* The Battered Women's Justice Project, 1801 Nicollet Ave., So., Suite 102, Minneapolis, MN 55403, technicalassistance@bwjp.org, 800.903.0111 prompt 1.

BWJP.org/files/bwjp/files/Mind_the_Gap_Accounting_for_Domes tic_Abuse_in_Child_Custody_Evaluations.pdf

30. Farney, A. C., and Valente, R. L. (2003). *Creating Justice Through Balance: Integrating Domestic Violence Law into Family Court Practice* Juvenile and Family Court Journal. Fall (Pg. 35-55). StopFamilyViolence.org/sites/documents/0000/0094/Valente_DV_ vs_FamilyCourt.pdf

31. Hardesty, J. L.; Khaw, L.; Chung, G. H.; Martin, J. M. (2008). *Coparenting Relationships after Divorce: Variations by Type of Marital Violence and Fathers' Role Differentiation,* Family Relations, 57(4), p. 479-491.

32. Scott, E. S. *Parental Autonomy and Children's Welfare,* 11 Wm. & Mary Bill of Rts. J. 1071 (2003), Scholarship.law.wm.edu/wmborj/vol11/iss3/6.

33. Zorza, J. (2010). *Parental Alienation Syndrome in Domestic violence, abuse, and child custody: Legal strategies and policy issues.* Hannah and Goldstein, (eds.). Civic Research Institute: Kingston, NJ.

34. Felitti, V.J., Anda, R.F., Nordenberg, D., Williamson, D.F., Spitz, A.M., Edwards, V., Koss, M.P., Marks, J.S. (1998). *Relationship of childhood abuse and household dysfunction to many of the leading causes of death in adults: The Adverse Childhood Experiences (ACE) Study.* American Journal of Preventive Medicine, 14:245–258. CDC.gov/ace/index.htm

35. The National Scientific Council on the Developing Child. (2003). *Toxic Stress: The Facts .* DdevelopingChild.harvard.edu/topics/science_of_early_childhood/ toxic_stress_response/

36. Walker, L.E.A., Cummings, D. M. & Cummings, N. A. (Eds.) (2012). *Our Broken Family Court System*. NY: Ithaca Press.

37. Katz J, Tirone, V. (2010).*Going along with it: Sexually coercive partner behavior predicts dating women's compliance with unwanted sex*. Violence Against Women, 16(7):730-42.

38. Shackelford, T. K. & Goetz, A. T. (2004). *Men's Sexual Coercion in Intimate Relationships: Development and Initial Validation of the Sexual Coercion in Intimate Relationships Scale*. Violence and Victims, 19 (5):541-556.

39. Martín, A.F., Vergeles, M.R., Acevedo, V. de L., Sánchez, A. del C., Visa, S.L. (2005). *The involvement in sexual coercive behaviors of Spanish college men: prevalence and risk factors*. Journal of Interpersonal Violence. 20(7):872-91.

40. Camilleri, J. A., Quinsey, V. L., & Tapscott, J. L. (2009). *Assessing the Propensity for Sexual Coaxing and Coercion in Relationships: Factor Structure, Reliability, and Validity of the Tactics to Obtain Sex Scale*. Archives of Sexual Behavior, 38:959–973.

41. Moore A.M., Frohwirth, L., Miller, E. (2010). *Male reproductive control of women who have experienced intimate partner violence in the United States*. Social Science and Medicine, 70(11):1737-44.

42. Hecht-Schafran, L. (2003). *Evaluating the Evaluators: Problems with 'Outside Neutral'"*, 42(1), Judges' Journal.

43. Miller, S.L., & Smolter, N. L. (2011). *"Paper abuse": when all else fails, batterers use procedural stalking*. Violence Against Women. 17(5):637-50. doi: 10.1177/1077801211407290. Epub 2011 Apr 28.

44.   Mouradian, V. E. (2011). *Abuse in Intimate Relationships: Defining the Multiple Dimensions and Terms.* National Violence Against Women Prevention Research Center, Wellesley Centers for Women, Wellesley College. Retrieved 4/17/2011 from Musc.edu/vawprevention/research/defining.shtml

45.   Araji, S. K. & Bosek, R. L. (2010). *Domestic Violence, Contested Child Custody, and the Courts: Findings from Five Studies* in Domestic violence, abuse, and child custody: Legal strategies and policy issues. Hannah and Goldstein, (eds.). Civic Research Institute: Kingston, NJ.

46.   Fulghum, Robert (1989). *All I Really Need to Know I Learned in Kindergarten.* (pg. 20), Villard Books: NY.

47.   Goldstein, B., & Liu, E. (2013). *Representing the Domestic Violence Survivor: Critical Legal Issues; Effective Safety Strategies.* Civic Research Institute: Kingston, NJ.

48.   Hannah, M. and Goldstein, B. (eds.). (2010). *Domestic violence, abuse, and child custody: Legal strategies and policy issues.* Civic Research Institute: Kingston, NJ.

49.   The state of New Hampshire governor's commission on domestic and sexual violence and attorney general's office faith communities: Domestic violence protocol (2007). Nhcadsv.org/uploads/faithbasedprotocol_2007.pdf

50.   Evans, P. (1993). *The Verbally Abusive Relationship: How to recognize it and how to respond.* Adams Media: Holbrook, MA.

51.   Engel, B. (2002). *The Emotionally Abusive Relationship: How to Stop Being Abused and How to Stop Abusing.* John Wiley & Sons, Inc.: NY.

52. Lehmann, P., Simmons, C.A., & Pillai, V. K. (2012). *The validation of the Checklist of Controlling Behaviors (CCB): Assessing coercive control in abusive relationships.* Violence Against Women, 18(8), 913-33.

53. Neustein, A. & Lesher, M. (2005). *From Madness to Mutiny: Why Mothers Are Running from the Family Courts -- and What Can Be Done about It.* Northeastern University Press: Lebanon, NH.

54. Holtzworth-Munroe, A.,. Beck, C. J. A and Applegate, A. G. (2010). *The mediator's assessment of safety issues and concerns (masic): A screening interview for intimate partner violence and abuse available in the public domain.* Family Court Review, 48(4), pgs. 646–662.

55. Johnson, Michael P. (2008). *A Typology of Domestic Violence: Intimate Terrorism, Violent Resistance, and Situational Couple Violence.* Boston, MA: Northeastern University Press.

Join your Voice with the Voices of Other Mothers

See Appendix C for books Protective Mothers have written. Truly it is: Maternal Deprivation Inflicted on Battered Women and Abused Children.

Maternal Deprivation, or Motherlessness, is occurring with alarming frequency due to the unethical treatment of women and children in family court. Go to this link to read more: LeadershipCouncil.org/1/pas/DVP.html

Family Court -- Unconstitutional Judicial Gag Orders --Prompted by embarrassed officials who dislike scrutiny and criticism by internet bloggers in the wake of burgeoning out-of-control shoot-from-the-hip "therapeutic jurisprudence" in the family courts. These orders are ILLEGAL under the First Amendment as violations of the constitutional prohibition against prior restraint.

Appendix B:

Resources

National Domestic Violence Hotline
Domestic Violence Hotlines
1–800–799–SAFE (7233) or TTY 1–800–787–3224
TheHotline.org/get-help/
    They will get you connected directly to services in your area.

Note: It is important you know about all resources that can be used in your case, both favorably as well as unfavorably.

Websites about the crisis in custody courts

Center for Judicial Excellence
CenterForJudicialExcellence.org

Justice for Children
JusticeForChildren.org

Leadership Council
LeadershipCouncil.org

Stop Family Violence
StopFamilyViolence.org

The Liz Library
TheLizLibrary.org

National Alliance for Family Court Justice (NAFC
Nafcj.net

Legal Resources
Locate attorneys through this directory
Martindale.com

American Bar Association
Mediation Information by state
*AmericanBar.org/content/dam/aba/migrated/domviol/docs/mediati
on_january_2008.authcheckdam.pdf*

American Bar Association
Guardian ad Litem

*AmericanBar.org/groups/probono_public_service/projects_award
s/child_custody_adoption_pro_bono_project.html*

American Bar Association
*AmericanBar.org/groups/probono_public_service/projects_award
s/child_custody_adoption_pro_bono_project.html*

See also: A Judge's Guide: Making Child Centered Decisions in
Custody Cases

DV LEAP
DVLeap.org
DV LEAP provides victims with the continued support needed to
take a case through the appellate process.

Domestic violence in Hague custody cases
(children taken to other countries)
HagueDV.org

Friend of the Court-Michigan
*NCDSV.org/images/MJI_FriendOfTheCourtDVResourceBook_201
2.pdf*

Parenting Coordination

American Psychological Association
Parenting Coordination Guidelines
APA.org/practice/guidelines/parenting-coordination.pdf

The Liz Library on Parenting Coordination
TheLizLibrary.org/site-index/site-index-frame.html#soulhttp://www.thelizlibrary.org/parenting-coordination/

American Psychological Association
Custody Evaluation Guidelines
APAPracticeCentral.org/news/guidelines.pdf

Association of Family and Conciliation Courts (AFCC) Standards and Guidelines in multiple areas including attorney representation in child custody cases
AFCCNET.org/ResourceCenter/PracticeGuidelinesandStandards

AFCC Model Standards in Child Custody
AFCCNET.org/Portals/0/ModelStdsChildCustodyEvalSept2006.pdf

Domestic Violence Resources online

National Network to End Domestic Violence
NNEDV.org

A project of *NNEDV*, providing legal information and support to victims of domestic violence and sexual assault
WomensLaw.org

Helpful information about Financial abuse and how to take back your life financially
NNEDV.org/projects/ecojustice.html

National Organization on Officer-Involved Domestic Violence
NOOIDV.org

More about domestic violence in law enforcement:
BehindTheBlueWall.blogspot.com/

Battered Women's Justice Project (Child Custody)
BWJP.org/custody.aspx

Child Development Information

Centers for Disease Control and Prevention
CDC.gov/ncbddd/childdevelopment/index.html

Search Institute
Search-Institute.org

Character Counts

CharacterCounts.org

Power and Control Wheels/Non-Violence Wheels

This site has many wheels that you may find helpful in your situation. *NCDSV.org/publications_wheel.html*

Appendix C:

Books

Books by Dr. Debra Wingfield

You may be wondering how you can learn more about Transformational Journaling™ and how you can use it to heal from any type of abuse. Check out the book

From Darkness to Light: Your Inner Journey
HouseOfPeacePubs.com link to products

For information on how you can help your children heal from being required to live with an abusive parent, check out the book

Through a Child's Voice: Transformational Journaling
HouseOfPeacePubs.com link to products

Books by other authors—check online bookstores

McLean, Maralee (2013). *Prosecuted but Not Silenced.* Tate Publishing

Rosen, Leora N. and Michelle Etlin (1996). *The Hostage Child: Sex Abuse Allegations in Custody Disputes,* Indiana University Press.

Swithin, Tina (2012). *Divorcing a Narcissist: One Mom's Battle.* Create Space.

Connect with Dr. Debra

Here's how to find me on the various social networks:

Blog: HouseOfPeacePubs.com

LinkedIn: linkedin.com/in/drdebra/

Twitter: @DrDebraW Twitter.com/DrDebraW

Facebook: Facebook.com/dr.debra.wingfield

YouTube Channel: YouTube.com/DrDebra

Amazon Profile: DrDebraWingfield.com/amazonprofile

Goodreads: AskDrDebra.com/goodreads

I can speak to your book group or organization anywhere in the world through the magic of technology. Contact me at info@houseofpeacepubs.com or call 1-719-647-0652.

How Dr. Debra Wingfield can help you:

Free Monthly Question and Answer (Q&A) calls
HouseOfPeacePubs.com, go to: AskDrDebraW

Debra A. Wingfield, Ed.D.

How to Share This Book with Your Friends & Colleagues

If this book has inspired and motivated you, chances are excellent that it is just what some of your friends and colleagues are seeking. So would you do me a favor and please take a few seconds to share this book and a quick review with them?

We've made it super simple. Just go to the Amazon.com page for Eyes Wide Open: Help! *with* Control Freak Co-Parents

Once on the Amazon Page, you'll notice **social sharing** buttons for your favorite networks below the "buy box."

Want to write a review? That would be most welcome.

Made in the USA
Middletown, DE
14 November 2020